# Haydn

*Reba Paeff Mirsky*

ILLUSTRATED BY W. T. MARS

*Follett Publishing Company   Chicago / New York*

*Books by Reba Paeff Mirsky*

NOMUSA AND THE NEW MAGIC

THIRTY-ONE BROTHERS AND SISTERS

SEVEN GRANDMOTHERS

BACH

BEETHOVEN

BRAHMS

MOZART

Library of Congress Catalog Card Number: 63-9612

SBN   695-43690-2   Titan binding
SBN   695-83690-0   Trade binding
        FOURTH PRINTING

*To Sonia and brother,*
*with much love*

*Chapter One*

$\mathcal{M}$ATTHIAS HAYDN and his
wife, Maria, sat by the large fireplace in their thatched cottage. Beside them were their five-year-old son, Joseph, and
his sister, Franziska, a year and a half older. Together they
were singing their favorite Austrian and Croatian folk songs
to the accompaniment of a small harp Matthias had bought
as a young man.

Although Father Haydn could not read a note of
music, he had learned to play the harp by ear. After the
day's work was done, the family enjoyed spending the evening singing together. Often little Joseph wanted to ask if
he might play the cherished instrument, but he did not dare.
Tonight, however, he was more courageous.

"Papa, may I try the harp now? I'll be very careful."

"No, Sepperl. It's much too old and delicate. You could easily break a string. Better take your two sticks and pretend they are a violin and bow. Some day we may be able to afford real ones for you."

Joseph's eyes shone at the prospect. He went to get his toy violin — two sticks of wood left over from the wagon spokes and wheels that his father made for a living. The child tucked one stick under his chin; with the other he bowed in perfect rhythm to the singing of his mother and father and Franziska, moving his fingers nimbly up and down on the neck of the imaginary violin.

When the children had gone to bed, Matthias said to his wife, "Maria, have you noticed how musical our Sepperl is?"

"Yes, I have. What a keen ear he has! And his memory is like glue. He never forgets a tune once he has heard it."

"Perhaps with his musical ability he would be accepted for training as a schoolteacher when he is older. It would be nice if he could do work that required his brains more than his hands," said his father.

"Good Heavens, Matthias, what is shameful about working with one's hands?" asked Maria indignantly. "Does anyone respect you the less for being the best wagonmaker and wheelwright in Rohrau? I am sure God does not despise

those who have less education so long as they are honest, work hard, and do not forget to pray." Sepperl's mother was a deeply religious woman.

She paused and continued, "I was thinking myself, though, how pleased I should be if our son were to become a priest."

"Well, when the day comes for such a decision, I won't stand in his way, and we can help him choose. Before long my cousin Franck is coming here from Hainburg. We can talk over Sepperl's education with him then."

"Yes, of course, he is a schoolmaster," said Maria.

"And he is also choirmaster of the Church of St. Philip and St. James. I hope he can tell us what to do about Sepperl's schooling. I'm afraid there isn't much that can be done for a bright lad in our little village."

"I am so glad he is coming," said Maria. "I shall bake good things for him to eat."

"All your baking is fit for a lord," said Matthias. "The great folks at the castle lost one of their best cooks when you married me."

Sepperl and Franziska were very much excited at the prospect of having a guest in the house. Hainburg was only four leagues from Rohrau, about two hours by coach, but it seemed very far away to them, and they thought of it as an especially exciting place because their father had been brought up there. They regarded Cousin Franck with awed interest and were on their very best behavior.

It did not take long for Cousin Franck to discover how musical Sepperl was. "Why don't you let me take the boy back with me to Hainburg?" he said to Maria and Matthias. "He won't be very far from home, and he can get a proper education and good musical training there. It won't cost much. Just enough for his board with my family and a small amount for school tuition."

Maria bit her lip and became solemn; then she said, "Thank you, Cousin, but I think our Sepperl is still too young to go away from home. It is very kind of you, but he is only five. Anyway, I want him to have the kind of schooling that would lead to his becoming a priest."

"Even if he were to become a priest," said Cousin Franck, "his training in music would not be a waste."

"We'll have to think it over a bit," said Matthias. "You know how it is with a mother. Sepperl is her only son now, and Maria can't bear to part with him, particularly because she lost so many of her other babies. Before you leave, though, we'll decide one way or the other."

The longer Cousin Franck remained with the Haydns, the more he was impressed by Sepperl's musical ability and intelligence. Every evening they sang together, Cousin Franck, Matthias, Maria and Franziska, and Sepperl, the little boy fiddling in perfect rhythm on his two sticks, at the same time singing in a piping clear voice.

"I hope you're not going to let your wonderful little son be wasted in this village," Cousin Franck said to Matthias.

The evening before Cousin Franck was to leave, after the children had gone to bed, Matthias said, "Cousin, my wife and I have decided."

Maria looked into the huge fireplace, her eyes swimming with tears. Cousin Franck had no doubt what the decision was, even before Matthias told him that Sepperl would go with him to Hainburg.

"It is for the best, dear Cousins, and you will never regret it. My wife and I will love him like one of our own children, and we will do everything to nourish his talent as well as his body. Have you told Sepperl yet?"

"Yes," said Maria, trying to be brave. "After his prayers, before he went to bed, I asked him, 'How should you like to go back with Cousin Franck and be in his school?' And he asked me, 'Will I be able to play a real violin there?' When I said I thought he would, he exclaimed, 'Then of course I want to go, Mama!' "

*Chapter Two*

N̊EXT MORNING Sepperl could hardly eat his breakfast because of his excitement. His mother saw that he was not at all sad about leaving home, and he did not notice the unhappy expression on her face as she hovered over him. When Sepperl saw the coach for Hainburg and its two prancing dappled horses, his delight was overwhelming.

He could hardly wait to be released from his parents' and sister's embraces and kisses, he was so eager to get into the coach and be off. Very soon the coach left behind the flat marshes and thatched clay houses of Rohrau and the winding Leitha River, the boundary between Hungary and Austria. Before long the road began to wind through the mountains that slope down to the Danube River, and Sepperl saw huge rocks and boulders, dense woods, ruined castles. So many wonderful things to see! Sepperl had meant to ask all about school, but he found himself too much taken up with the excitement of what he was seeing. It didn't seem like two hours later when Cousin Franck said, "We're almost there, Sepperl. Right ahead of us are the ancient gates of Hainburg." He began gathering up their belongings.

"What high towers on the walls!" exclaimed Sepperl admiringly.

"In the old days every town was a fortress, and border towns more than most. Your father can remember when those old walls served well against the Hungarian rebels, and before that it was the Turks. There are even the marks of bullets on the gate."

Sepperl gazed at the old fortress town with increased respect. Then he turned and looked up at Cousin Franck, his eyes shining with delight, and said, "I didn't know Hainburg would be like this."

"Just wait until you see how beautiful the church of St. Philip and St. James is," said his cousin proudly.

When they had got out of the coach, Sepperl asked, "What do you do in the church, Cousin?"

"I have charge of the music. I play the organ, train the singers, and show the musicians how to play the various instruments. At school I have two assistants to help me teach the eighty children reading, writing, arithmetic, singing, and prayers."

"You must be very busy," said Sepperl.

"Indeed I am! Besides all that, I have to keep the church register, look after the church clock, and ring the bells for services and for thunderstorms and fires."

"Oh, I'll be glad to help you with the bells," said Sepperl enthusiastically.

"Yes, but I'd have to make the bell ropes much longer," said Cousin Franck, with a laugh. "However, you'll have plenty to do without bell ringing. I don't think I've told you about the hours you'll keep. School begins at seven in the morning and lasts until mass, at ten. At eleven the boys go home for lunch.

"From twelve to three there is school again. After that, homework and music lessons. After a while you can copy music for me and sing in the choir. In a few weeks I'll give you lessons on the violin and the harpsichord. Would you like that?"

"Oh, yes, Cousin Franck. As soon as we can!"

A few months later Matthias went to Hainburg to see how Sepperl was getting on and to bring him news from home.

Hugging his little son, Matthias said, "I have a surprise for you — not in these packages, though."

"Where is it, then?" asked Sepperl eagerly.

"At home, with your mother."

"Did you forget it, Papa?"

"It's a baby brother!" announced Matthias.

Sepperl was overjoyed. "What's his name?"

"Michael — Johann Michael. He seems a strong healthy boy."

"Oh, do bring him here with Mama and Franziska next time."

"When he's a little older, perhaps. Now let me show you the good things your mother has been cooking for you."

Next spring, Sepperl's father came to Hainburg in Holy Week and found that Sepperl was to take the part of a drummer who had died just before the festival. He had been practicing so energetically that Cousin Franck's wife could hardly bear it, but Cousin Franck was pleased at how quickly he had learned.

Matthias made sure he got a good place from which to see the procession, and he looked eagerly for the musicians. Sure enough, there was Sepperl, striding along the cobbled street behind a short hunchback to whose back the drum was strapped so he could reach it. Sepperl pounded with such enthusiasm and in such perfect rhythm that Matthias could hardly keep from laughing out loud. He was proud of his little son. What a feeling for rhythm the lad had!

Later, when Matthias was taking the coach back to Rohrau, Sepperl said, "Please tell Mama I thank her for all

*14*

the good things she sent me; give my kisses to Franziska and little Michael. And don't forget to tell them I know how to play the drum."

"Certainly I'll tell them. But I'm sure your mother will be very glad you're not making all that noise at home."

Then he asked softly, so no one would hear, "Sepperl, are you getting enough to eat at Cousin Franck's? You're not very fat now, and Mama would worry. Please don't give away all the cheese and sausage and cookies she sent you; eat a good share of them yourself, you hear?"

"Yes, Papa, but the other children will like them, too. It wouldn't be nice to keep everything for myself."

The coach was ready to go. Matthias hugged Sepperl and got inside. The horses galloped off. Sepperl waved until the coach was out of sight; then he ran back to Cousin Franck's house. He was greeted by the noise and crying of his cousin's two small children, the youngest only a baby. Juliane Rosine, Cousin Franck's wife, was constantly busy with her babies, and there was no one to help her except Sepperl.

It had gradually dawned on Sepperl that his cousins were too poor to hire outside help. Rosine was depending on Sepperl as if he were the oldest of her children, the one she could ask to help her with household chores, to look after the babies and run errands for her.

Luckily Sepperl had been brought up to help his

mother. Still, he could not help comparing his Aunt Rosine's slovenliness with his mother's perfect housekeeping. He remembered how his mother had scrubbed his clothes and body so that he was spotless. Rosine had no time to notice or care whether he was clean, whether his clothes were washed or mended. She had her hands full without looking after his needs too. He was dreadfully ashamed of all the dirty spots on his clothes, and hoped his father had not noticed.

At any rate, to Sepperl, the advantages of being in school at Hainburg more than made up for the neglect and lack of peace in the Franck household. He enjoyed all the special occasions when religious and town events were celebrated with splendid pageantry and music. It was thrilling to see the civil guards in their brilliant uniforms playing fanfares on trumpets and drums from the high altar of the church before mass.

He loved being part of the processions and the choir music. The choirboys were just as necessary as the grown-up singers and musicians. Young Franz Joseph Haydn had a profession already; and when he stood up in the choir to sing, wearing a little powdered wig for cleanliness, he felt quite like a little man. And how much he was learning!

## Chapter Three

ORE THAN a year had gone by since Sepperl had come to Hainburg. His voice was getting stronger and purer; and he was now considered one of the best singers in the choir, and people were beginning to notice him.

One thing disturbed Sepperl. Cousin Franck was growing more and more irritable and impatient with his pupils. No one knew better than Sepperl that it was because he was overworked, taking on extra jobs in order to support his family. Poor Cousin Franck! thought Sepperl, with crowded quarters at home, no peace or rest because of the babies, and constant worry about making ends meet.

No wonder he lost his temper easily and often caned

the boys. Sepperl got his share with the others. One day a choirboy told him, "Your sour old cousin may beat us, but he is forbidden to pull our hair. He'll get into trouble with the town council if he tries *that*."

Despite Cousin Franck's severity, and the fact that he was often dirty and was not getting enough to eat, Sepperl's disposition remained so sweet, his delight in his music lessons was so great, that he was more than willing to put up with it all. As a matter of fact he felt he could not be grateful enough for what his cousin was doing for him.

Among the people who noticed Sepperl's singing was Pastor Palmb. One day he sent for the boy. Sepperl worked hard to wipe off the worst stains from his suit. As he energetically washed and scrubbed his hands and face, he wondered why Pastor Palmb wanted to see him. Had he done something wrong? He'd certainly catch it from Cousin Franck. He hurried to the pastor's house, his skin aglow from the scrubbing.

In Pastor Palmb's house, Sepperl saw an important-looking stranger. Bowing to him and the pastor, he said, "Good day to you, sirs."

"Sepperl, I am glad to see you," said the pastor kindly. "I want this gentleman, Herr Karl Reutter, to hear you sing. He is choirmaster of the famous St. Stephen's Cathedral in Vienna, as well as official court composer. He is looking for a boy to sing in his choir. I told him you have quite a good voice, though it is still a bit weak, and he wants to hear you."

Sepperl shyly smiled at Herr Reutter.

"How old are you, my boy?" asked the choirmaster.

"Going on eight, sir."

"Very good. Do you think you could sing this piece of music?"

Sepperl looked at the piece of music for a moment. It was a song he had never heard. Reutter noticed his surprised look and said, "Go ahead, boy. Of course you don't know this song, but try reading it. You should learn to read music at sight the way a person reads a book."

"I'll try, sir," said Sepperl.

He began singing the song with such beauty and accuracy that Pastor Palmb and Herr Reutter exchanged glances of approval.

When Sepperl finished singing, he said, "That's a beautiful song, sir."

"You didn't sing it at all badly, Joseph," said Herr Reutter, "but you don't seem to know how to trill when it is required. Why is that?"

"Perhaps because Cousin Franck hasn't taught me, sir. I don't think he knows how to, either."

Pastor Palmb looked away to hide his amused smile.

"Come closer, lad," said the choirmaster, "and I'll teach you how to sing a trill."

He took Sepperl between his knees and showed him

how to sing notes in rapid succession, and how to control his breath. "Look into my mouth and see how I use the palate to make the trill," he said.

Sepperl learned the trick quickly, and soon produced such a splendid trill that the delighted choirmaster emptied the plate of cherries on the table into his hands, saying, "You're a clever lad."

"Oh, thank you very much! From now on, I'll never make a trill without thinking of these lovely cherries."

"Now, Joseph, if your parents agree, you can come to Vienna and be in my choir at St. Stephen's, where you will have the finest musical education to be had in Austria. It's a great honor to be chosen; we take only six boys. They are trained in the choir school and sing in the cathedral choir. Should you like to be one of them?"

"Certainly, Herr Reutter, if my mother and father and Cousin Franck are willing," said Sepperl joyfully.

"Well, I shall go and see them, and if they do not object, I'll make the arrangements. When will you be eight?"

"On March 31st, sir. I was born in 1732."

"Then you will not be eight till next spring. We don't take boys until they are at least eight. In the meantime, practice hard, singing scales. Try reading songs you never heard anyone sing, and train your ear to recognize tones and chords; that's how your voice and ear will improve. If your cousin is too busy to help you, work by yourself. You're a clever boy, and you can make progress that way."

"I'll work hard, sir," promised Sepperl. "I do hope my parents will say yes!"

"I rather think they will. I'll send word to your cousin and the pastor after I have seen them. Shall I tell your parents you send greetings?"

"Of course! Please excuse me for forgetting. And I send kisses to Franziska and my little brother."

"You have a little brother? Perhaps he too will be a singer some day," said Herr Reutter.

"He is sure to be, sir. We all love to sing at home."

There was a new baby in the Franck family that autumn and Sepperl was kept even busier than before; but he practiced and studied every day, and he knew that he was improving. The last few months flew by. Matthias came to Hainburg to celebrate Sepperl's eighth birthday with him and help him get ready for his trip to Vienna. When the time came for him to leave, his father and Cousin Franck saw Sepperl off. His father hugged him, saying, "Take good care of yourself, my son, and let us hear from you often. If you need anything, let us know."

"Thank you, Papa; my love to Mama, Franziska, and Michael. Many thanks to you, too, Cousin Franck. I hope Aunt Rosine will soon find someone else to help her."

The trip to Vienna took several hours; Sepperl was so interested that he wished it had been longer. Gazing through the window at the ever-changing countryside, watching farmers ploughing their fields, seeing cows and chickens standing in barnyards, he was never bored for a moment.

At Vienna, Herr Reutter and the five other choirboys were waiting for the coach. The boys were friendly, and full of helpful information.

Now Sepperl was able to see the famous cathedral and the choir house beside it that would be his home for the next ten years. One of the boys told him, "I bet you never saw a spire like the one on our cathedral here. It was built over four hundred years ago."

Sepperl gazed at the steeple and the roof with its colored tiles and innumerable statues. The tall spire was slender and delicate like a piece of beautiful lace. He could hardly wait to see what the cathedral was like inside.

After a meagre supper, he learned that Herr Reutter and his three assistants were responsible for the education and musical training of the choirboys, but that they had many other duties as well. The boys told him that Herr Reutter received 1200 florins a year (the florin was worth about fifty cents) from the City of Vienna, and out of this amount he had to provide the choirboys with food and clothing.

"What do they teach us?" asked Sepperl.

"They teach us religion, Latin — all the regular school subjects — and the violin, harpsichord, and singing."

Because of the gift of cherries at Pastor Palmb's house,

Sepperl had expected Herr Reutter to be a kind, generous person. It did not take him long to discover that this was not entirely so.

To his surprise he found that the choirmaster was even more severe than Cousin Franck, and in addition there was even less food than Aunt Rosine had been able to provide. For the first time Sepperl really felt pangs of hunger. His thoughts began to linger more on food than on music.

One day when he was complaining to one of the older choirboys about how hungry he was, the boy told him, "Listen, Joseph, tomorrow we are giving a concert at a nobleman's house. There are always wonderful things to eat afterwards. Sometimes it's a regular feast. That's your chance to fill up."

"Are there such concerts often?" asked Sepperl.

"Yes, but they usually don't invite all the boys — just the ones who are the best singers."

"I see!" said Sepperl thoughtfully. He determined that whenever the choirboys were invited to sing at the homes of the Viennese nobility, he would sing as beautifully as he could, so that they would remember to ask for him next time.

And remember him they did, to the delight of his rumbling stomach. Moreover, the baker near St. Stephen's, who came to the cathedral services, was so pleased with Sepperl's singing that he always gave him a cake as a present when he passed his bakeshop.

*Chapter Four*

ACH DAY Sepperl and the choir boys sang for the two services at St. Stephen's. They were also in the Cathedral at other times to practice. Sepperl had plenty of time to get acquainted with every part of the beautiful building.

The choirboys sang not only at the daily services but also at special services during Holy Week, on feast days, royal birthdays, at funerals and pageants. Whenever there was a large sacred choral composition to be performed that required boys' voices as well as men's, they sang also at the royal court.

With so many occasions to sing different kinds of music, Sepperl gradually became acquainted with the music of composers he had never heard of before. He was very eager to learn and was always attentive, especially since his teachers were too busy to give him much help. At the choir school his musical studies were chiefly singing and the playing of musical instruments, with no encouragement to learn anything else. But making music was what Sepperl enjoyed most, and so long as he could remain in Vienna and take part in the Cathedral services, processions, and pageants, he was happy. There were many wonderful pageants. The Emperor Charles VI died in the October of Sepperl's first year in Vienna, and there was a state funeral followed by a splendid coronation ceremony. There were celebrations when each of the royal children were born and baptized and others connected with the war. But the coronation was the best.

Charles VI's daughter Maria Theresa could not inherit her father's rank as Holy Roman Emperor. That was an elective title, not hereditary. The electors, who were German princes, usually chose the ruler of Austria; but Maria Theresa was not eligible because she was a woman. But she inherited the Hapsburg family lands — if she could keep them from the many other possible heirs who had promised her father to respect her rights but who might find it convenient to break their promises. She was Archduchess of Austria and Queen of Hungary and of Bohemia, besides ruling over the Austrian lands in Italy and the Netherlands. The most memorable procession Sepperl ever saw was for her Austrian coronation. The coronation took place at the Burg, the castle, and the procession went from there to the Cathedral, where there would be a religious ceremony.

The choir boys were assigned a special place near the Cathedral so that they could get in easily and be ready when they were needed. But what crowds! There were people in the streets, on roofs, on balconies, on iron fences and lamp posts, small children sitting on their fathers' shoulders.

Soldiers in white uniforms and three-cornered hats lined the route of the parade. The streets were decorated, and flags fluttered in the cold November winds.

Sepperl had a hard time seeing anything, but he managed to squeeze between two fat women and get a better view. Suddenly there was a roar of intense excitement that rumbled like a wave over a wide-swept beach. Sepperl was beside himself with excitement. He hoped he would see the beautiful Maria Theresa through the window of her royal carriage. It seemed strange that a woman could be their sovereign.

First came all sorts of great dignitaries in rich robes, then the royal bearers carrying the Archduke's hat, which was in Austria what crowns were in other countries. And then came the new Archduchess! Not in a carriage at all but in a glass-windowed sedan chair, carried by strong men in splendid uniforms, steadily and evenly so there would be no jolting. Behind her came the great state coach, empty, drawn by six sleek black Spanish horses. The Archduchess could look out at her admiring people through the glass sides of the chair, and they could see her as well.

She was resplendent in a heavy silk gown trimmed with ermine. Diamonds glittered from her powdered hair, and each flat curl was neatly and artistically arranged over her head and plump neck. Sepperl thought her magnificent, but rather fat. Twenty-three seemed rather old to him; and besides, she was a wife and a mother. She looked firm and capable and good-humored, as if she would be a nice mother to have. One of the women next to Sepperl said that she rode in a chair because she was going to have another baby. "It would not be safe for her to ride in the royal carriage, bumped over the cobblestones."

The other said, "Yes, but I do worry about her bare neck and arms. She could catch her death of cold in this weather."

It *was* cold, and Sepperl was not sorry to be hurried into the Cathedral with the other choirboys. As he went in he suddenly remembered that he had not even thought of Maria Theresa's husband, the Grand Duke Francis, and decided to look for him at the ceremony. He was probably not worth looking at compared to his wife, but she loved him dearly, everyone said, and was going to make him her co-ruler.

The cathedral organ burst into jubilant music and Sepperl prepared to sing. But there was so much to look at!

Indeed, he was so busy looking at the dignitaries in their gorgeous robes that he almost forgot to sing when Herr Reutter gave the signal. The choirmaster scowled at him angrily. He had brought that boy to Vienna to sing, not to gape at everything like a country bumpkin!

That winter the war began. It seemed to Sepperl that every Prince in the Empire and half of the rest of Europe too was trying to get part of Maria Theresa's dominions. At first things looked dangerously bad, but then there began to be celebrations of victories. In 1745, when Sepperl was thirteen, Maria Theresa's husband was elected Holy Roman Emperor, and Vienna celebrated, although the coronation would be at Frankfort. The war was not yet over, but it meant a great deal to the Austrians to have an Emperor again — and to have their beloved Maria Theresa an Empress.

In the meanwhile Sepperl was learning as much as he could and wishing it were more. Reutter was not interested in the general education of his choirboys, and gave them only enough musical education to make them better choirboys. What he wanted from them was that they become expert singers and sight readers and learn to play an instrument passably well, either the harpsichord or violin, or both.

Sepperl yearned to learn something about the grammar of music, about music theory. Then he would be able to write music. He was full of musical ideas and was already working on a piece for twelve voices. When Herr Reutter came upon him trying to write it out, he laughed. "See here, silly boy, aren't two parts enough for you? If you're so anxious to write music, you can arrange the motets we sing in church. But I tell you in advance I have absolutely no time to correct your mistakes."

"I don't want to be extra trouble to you, sir. I know you are terribly busy," said Sepperl.

"I'm sure you have no idea *how* busy I am," said Herr Reutter irritably. "I hope you choristers appreciate the great advantage you have because I am conductor and composer to the royal court as well as director of the Cathedral choir. When you are invited to sing with royal chapel singers, you hear many wonderful compositions."

"Is it true, Herr Reutter, that our Empress is a very good singer herself?" asked Sepperl.

"Yes, and a great connoisseur of music. She has studied with famous teachers and can instantly judge fine musicianship. We have been invited to sing at her newly remodeled summer palace at Schönbrunn. They say the grounds and gardens are magnificent. I hope you boys will be on your best behavior and not disgrace me in any way."

Soon the day came for the choirboys to be taken to the Empress Maria Theresa's summer palace. Their coach drove through the palace gate, which was crowned with gilt eagles and guarded by stone sphynxes. They saw ahead of them a vast, yellow, sprawling building that seemed to have hundreds of rooms. A splendid sweeping outdoor staircase ascended to the entrance. The boys gazed in wonder at the ponds, with the ducks and swans, the high hedges fashioned of trees, the fountains and statues all about the gardens, the hothouse with its rare plants.

Unfortunately, the wooden scaffolding had not yet been removed from one side of the enlarged palace, and the sight of it tempted the repressed choirboys beyond endurance. When Herr Reutter went indoors, the boys began climbing over the scaffolding with shouts of glee.

It was exactly the kind of physical exercise they needed and longed for, and they were enjoying themselves tremendously. Suddenly they heard a sharp rapping on a window near them. It was the Empress herself, commanding them to get down at once.

The boys scrambled to the ground as swiftly as monkeys, wondering what the choirmaster would do to them if he heard about it. When they were called in to sing, they outdid themselves, hoping that the Empress would forget to report them. No one mentioned their misbehavior, and they returned to Vienna delighted with the outing.

Next day they were invited again to come and sing for the Empress at Schönbrunn. Once more they gazed at the tempting scaffolding, but they were determined to resist their desire to climb it.

Excepting Sepperl. He glanced at the palace windows to make sure the Empress wasn't watching, then began climbing. The boys called warningly, "Joseph, you'd better not! You'll get into awful trouble if you're caught."

But Sepperl kept on climbing, his cheeks flushed with the pleasure of doing something forbidden. The release from Herr Reutter's severe discipline, the chance to use his arms and legs, was worth any punishment that would follow.

It was the Empress herself who caught him at it. She suddenly appeared at a window and called sternly, "Get down at once, you blond blockhead! I'll see to it that Herr Reutter gives you what you deserve."

Quickly Sepperl slid down, almost tumbling into the arms of the frightened choirboys. Now he had got them all into trouble. Sheepishly they answered the summons to come and sing in the palace. Never did they sing better.

The Empress had for some time noticed how beautifully Sepperl sang his solos; but that did not prevent her from being as good as her word when — as he had to admit — he deserved it. Sepperl got his thrashing; but later in life he was rather proud to tell of it.

In September of the year Sepperl was thirteen, his brother Michael was eight — old enough to get into the choir school if he could pass the test. When he was accepted, Sepperl's joy was unbounded.

*Chapter Five*

**A**FTER BEING away from his family so long, Sepperl was delighted that his younger brother, whom he hardly knew, was coming to the choir school. And when Michael arrived, Sepperl was even more delighted. He thought him the cleverest, the best singer, the most musical of all the choristers.

Everyone began saying, "What a remarkable voice the new choirboy has. How attractive and intelligent he is, far more than his big brother." Instead of this making Sepperl jealous or resentful, it made him proud and happy. And since Herr Reutter and his assistants were too busy to give Michael regular music lessons, Sepperl began teaching him everything he knew.

Michael learned quickly; and although he was only a little boy whose feet could hardly reach the organ pedals, of all the instruments he enjoyed the organ most. Before long he became so good at it that he was able to earn a little money occasionally as a substitute organist at practice sessions. What he enjoyed especially was improvising and composing on the organ. The huge sounds reverberating through the lofty cathedral gave him a sense of power, as if he were commanding an orchestra. It seemed fantastic that those great sounds could be made by so small a boy.

Because of his high spirits, self-confidence, and ability, Michael became very popular with the other choirboys. Reutter was much pleased with him too. Michael had a beautiful voice, with a range of three octaves. Joseph's voice, on the other hand, was becoming untrustworthy in his adolescence. Once his voice broke when he was singing before the Empress, and she commented on it. She told the choirmaster that his soprano wasn't singing, he was crowing! The solos that Sepperl used to sing were now given to Michael, and Sepperl considered this the proper thing to do. He himself was none too pleased with the sound of his own singing. The Empress applauded his brother enthusiastically, and Sepperl's heart swelled with pride.

Late in 1748 the choristers of St. Stephen's gave a concert with the court chapel singers at a festival at the Klosterneuburg monastery in honor of the patron saint of Lower

Austria. Michael sang his solo so exquisitely that the Emperor and Empress sent for him after the performance and gave him a present of twenty-four golden ducats.

Herr Reutter asked him afterwards, "What do you intend to do with so much money, Michael?"

"I'll send half of it to my father because he just lost a cow. The other half, please keep for me until my voice breaks, like my brother's."

It pained Michael to see Herr Reutter's displeasure with Sepperl just because his voice was changing. Anyone could see that the choirmaster was looking for an excuse to get rid of him. Having an extra choirboy around who could neither sing properly nor play the violin or harpsichord outstandingly was so much money out of his pocket.

Sepperl was very unhappy. His father came up to Vienna expressly to tell him that he was glad his son was becoming a man. "Don't mind what Reutter says," said Matthias. "If he had his way, you'd still have a beautiful soprano voice when you were forty years old. And how would you like that?" Sepperl agreed that he wouldn't like it at all, and he felt much cheered. Still, his future as a choirboy was obviously going to be short.

In time, Sepperl knew, his voice would again become strong, and lower in tone, a man's voice; but now it was useless in the choir. As time went by and his voice did not improve in steadiness, Herr Reutter's irritation with him increased daily. It was obvious that he begrudged him the room he took up in his house, the food he ate at his table.

Sepperl was sure the axe would fall any day now. Full of foreboding, he waited anxiously, fearful of the future. He did not want to leave the choir school. He loved hearing the music at the cathedral and at the court, and it was a pleasure to play the violin and the harpsichord, even though he showed no remarkable talent on either of them. Besides, he wanted to be near Michael, whom he loved and was proud of.

Now that he was unable to sing in the rehearsals and performances, Sepperl had more time to think of naughty pranks. He had too much unused energy. One afternoon he found a new pair of scissors on a table in the choir house. Unfortunately, another choirboy was sitting in front of him, and quick as a wink Sepperl cut off the beribboned pigtail of his wig. It made Sepperl exceedingly cheerful to see what he had done. And somehow it also seemed to relieve his unhappy feelings and misgivings about the choirmaster.

As soon as Herr Reutter heard what Sepperl had done, he shouted at him, "That does it! You will be caned on the hand for that, young man."

"I won't allow it," declared Sepperl defiantly. "I am seventeen years old, and I'd rather leave than be caned."

"By all means, go. I can hardly wait. But only after you have been caned."

*36*

Sepperl was turned out of the choir school on a cold day in November. He had only the suit on his back and three shirts. There wasn't a penny in his pocket.

Michael was choked with unhappiness. He hoped the lump in his throat would disappear before he had to sing at the cathedral service.

Sepperl did not know what to do now, but of one thing he was sure: he would not go home and be a burden on his parents, or ask them to send him money until he found some kind of a job in Vienna. He knew that in two months his sister Franziska was to be married to the village baker and that his parents were having a hard enough time providing her with the expected dowry.

Unable to sing or to play a musical instrument well enough to be a soloist, with no letter of recommendation from Herr Reutter, Sepperl's prospects were bleak indeed. He wandered through the cold streets of Vienna, discouraged and anxious; that night he slept on a park bench. Next day a young man suddenly stopped him on the street and said, "Hello, Joseph. What are you doing around here?"

It was Johann Michael Spangler, who had been one of the older singers at the church in Hainburg when Sepperl was studying with Cousin Franck. Now he sang in the choir of St. Michael's Church. Noticing the worried expression on the boy's face, he asked, "Is something wrong?"

"I've lost my place in the choir school," Sepperl said,

feeling his friendliness. He told him about the trouble with his voice, about the unfortunate prank with the scissors.

"Where are you living?" asked Spangler.

"I'm not living anywhere at the moment. I was just wondering where to stay and how to find a musical job."

"Why not come and stay with me and my wife until you find something to do? We live in a poor little attic, and our nine-month-old baby may wake you up at night with his crying. Still, until you get a job, it's better than nothing. I'm not very well off myself so I can't offer to feed you; but at least you'll have a roof over your head for the time being."

"That's terribly kind of you, Spangler, and I really ought not to accept your offer, but I have no other place to go. I hope I won't have to impose on you for long. My heartfelt thanks!"

*Chapter Six*

$\mathcal{I}$T DID not take long for young Haydn to find small jobs playing the fiddle at dances, giving music lessons for very small fees, or taking part in serenades. The serenades were light music performed out of doors by several musicians playing different instruments. Serenaders were often hired by a suitor to compliment his lady and bring him her favor. Serenades were also performed to celebrate a birthday or wedding anniversary. Most of the music played was popular Viennese folk music, and enthusiastic crowds would gather to enjoy it.

The instruments had to be portable, so keyboard instruments and even the heavy bass violin had to be left out. Because of this there was no fundamental bass line to the music, making the light instrumentation appear to float in the air. Still, the music had to be strong enough so that the wind would not dispel its tone.

The usual instruments for outdoor music were flutes, oboes, violins, clarinets, and lutes, and the most common combination of them was two stringed instruments and a wind instrument. Serenading gave Haydn quite a different musical training and experience from what he had received as a choirboy. He enjoyed the lightweight popular music and the different combinations of musical instruments. It was fun to be in the midst of a throng of people hanging on every note they played, humming along, whistling, keeping time with hands or feet.

After living for several months with the Spanglers in their crowded attic, Haydn was able to tell them one day, "You have been very good to me, my friends. Now I can afford to get a place of my own so I shall move and give you the space I have taken up for the new baby you are expecting."

"We shall be sorry to see you go, Joseph. Where shall you live?"

"I have managed to find a tiny attic room, up six flights, in the old Michaelerhaus by St. Michael's church."

"Oh, yes — one of those tenement palaces."

"Exactly. Aristocracy on the first floor; middle class on the floors above; servants, tradespeople, and poor devils like me up under the roof. I hear the Dowager Princess Esterházy

occupies the first floor. Metastasio is on the third, the court poet and opera librettist. My neighbors on the top floor are a cook, a printer, and a footman."

"Is there a stove, so you can keep warm?" asked Frau Spangler solicitously.

"No," Haydn replied. "No stove, and I'll have to carry water up six flights from the well in the yard below. But I don't mind. I've managed to borrow 150 florins from the father of one of my pupils. Now I'll be able to get myself a worm-eaten little harpsichord I saw for sale, and some books that will teach me how to compose. I am going to enjoy my attic very much."

Haydn knew very well what he wanted to do with his life. He was a musician, and he intended to be a composer. But how could he be one when he did not know how to set down his musical thoughts? If only he had had some training for composing! He was like a person who wished to write a book but had never learned how to write sentences.

Soon Haydn was practicing on his worn-out little harpsichord and studying the books that he hoped would give him the necessary knowledge for composing. He worked his way steadily through the exercises in books on music theory. Best of all, one day he discovered the first six harpsichord sonatas by Carl Philipp Emanuel Bach, a son of old Johann Sebastian Bach's. He was so impressed by the sonatas that he told his friends the Spanglers, "These Bach sonatas have opened a new world to me. I play them over and over for my own delight, especially when I feel discouraged and worried. After playing them through I envy no king his happiness."

"That's not surprising," said Spangler. "Philipp Emanuel Bach always says, 'A musician cannot move others unless he himself is moved.' There have been plenty of others inspired by him."

Spangler's wife changed the subject — "Any new pupils lately?"

"Yes, one. She is a marvelous little Spanish girl, Marianne de Martinez, daughter of the Pope's ambassador, who lives in the same building I do. She is only nine years old and has tremendous talent. You should hear how she plays. Her quick notes hop like birds on a branch. I give her a music lesson every day."

"At any rate, you'll soon be rich."

"Oh, but I don't get paid in money. The family gives me free meals in exchange for the lessons. And I get more than that. The child is also studying singing and composition with that amazing Italian teacher and composer, Porpora. He has me accompany her during the singing lessons, and I am learning a great deal that I need to know by being there."

"I can't say I envy you your association with that irritable old fellow," said Spangler. "He must be seventy."

"It doesn't matter in the least to me that he's old and irritable. Porpora is a remarkable teacher, a master of melody. He can give me such a good foundation in composition that I have asked him to take me with him as his valet this summer. He is going to Mannersdorf and will live with the Venetian ambassador."

"You intend to go as his servant!" exclaimed Spangler. "I wouldn't have believed it of you."

"I wouldn't do it for anyone else, but he'll correct my compositions and give me lessons in singing and in Italian in exchange. He is a great musician, and I can learn a lot from him."

"You won't be very far from home, either."

"Only about twenty miles. I intend to go to see my father whenever I can. I wish my dear mother were still alive. But I suppose I should be glad at least that she lived till Michael and I were old enough to visit her. It was wonderful to gather around and sing to my father's harp as we used to do when we were little."

At the end of three months Haydn was back in Vienna. He went to see his good friends again as soon as he returned.

"How did you get along with the old bear?" they asked, full of curiosity.

"I must admit he's a difficult, bad-tempered fellow and treated me none too well. He often called me insulting names, and he didn't spare his slaps, either; but I learned so much from him that it was worth it. At such a fashionable summer resort, I was able to hear many remarkable concerts, too; and I even met the famous composer, Gluck. He was very encouraging and kind. He urged me to continue my studies in Italy. I can't afford to go, of course, but still, it was nice to be told I ought to. Perhaps some day I may."

"You certainly have more patience and determination than I suspected," said Spangler, shaking his head. "Cleaning shoes and brushing clothes for that cranky old bear! But still, you did get good instruction out of him and got acquainted with other musicians."

With the knowledge of composition that he was getting from Porpora and from studying the books he had bought, Haydn began to feel better equipped to go ahead with some harpsichord sonatas he was composing. These turned out so well that Haydn used them with his students. One day the Countess Thun, a fine musician, heard a friend play them and said, "I should very much like to meet the composer of these lovely sonatas. Is it possible?"

It was arranged, and young Haydn arrived at the appointed time. He felt very awkward when the beautifully dressed countess came forward to greet him. She, in turn, had to hide her surprise at finding him so young and so shabby. He was not tall, and his face was pitted with scars from the smallpox, but she liked his kindly gray eyes, so full of humor. "Herr Haydn," she said, "I have very much enjoyed your beautiful sonatas. I wonder if you have time to give me singing and harpsichord lessons."

Haydn was delighted at the opportunity. He told the Spanglers proudly of his new pupil, who was well known in Vienna as one of the most accomplished of the many music-loving nobles.

"You're certainly in luck, Joseph. The Countess Thun has many musical friends among the nobility. In time they may take an interest in your compositions," said Spangler.

Sure enough, one of Countess Thun's friends, the Baron Karl von Fürnberg, engaged Haydn as music teacher for his family and later took him to his country estate in the mountains, about sixty miles from Vienna, to play chamber music and continue teaching the family. The musicians with whom he played liked Haydn's music. He wrote his first string quartet there, and they praised it so warmly that he immediately set to work to compose others for them to play.

From now on, because so many pupils wished him to be their teacher, he was able to charge more for his music lessons. He also got other musical jobs, and soon he found himself often working sixteen to eighteen hours a day, especially on Sundays.

In the morning he would play the violin at a church; from there he went to the private chapel of a nobleman to play the organ. Afterwards he went to sing tenor parts at the cathedral, for now he had a good singing voice again. And every day there were music lessons to be given at the homes of his pupils.

He returned home late at night, his legs ready to collapse from all the walking he had to do to get to his various jobs and pupils, ending up with the six-flight climb to his attic. To rest himself he often went to his friend and comforter, his harpsichord, to practice and compose.

He could feel the weariness leave his body as he sat working at his beloved music. It was wonderful to be able to earn his living at something he so much liked to do.

By now Michael had also reached the age when his voice was changing. He too was no longer useful at the choir school and had to leave — without the money he had asked Herr Reutter to save for him. Reutter couldn't remember a thing about it. Michael was more fortunate than his brother had been, however, for he immediately found good musical jobs in Hungary. When he was only twenty, he got a permanent appointment. Before taking it he came back to Vienna and visited his brother.

"Well, Sepperl, I'm certainly in luck. I shall be conductor to the noble Bishop of Grosswardein."

"Wonderful, Michael!"

"Yes, it is. I never would have had your courage to stay and make my way in Vienna, where the competition is so keen. I see you are beginning to get somewhere here, and I am very thankful. But how overworked you look!"

"Oh, it's nothing; don't worry about me, Michael. I am only too glad to have the work. Of course, I'd rather have one good job that would support me than a lot of little ones that are uncertain and keep me going from morning to night, but I think my prospects of finding one are getting better all the time."

But it was two years before Haydn was able to tell his friends the Spanglers that he had been offered a good position through the recommendation of the Baron von Fürnberg.

"What kind of a position is it?"

"Music director and composer for Count Morzin. He and his wife are deeply interested in music and have their own orchestra of sixteen musicians. They have a winter home in Vienna, so I shall not be stuck in Bohemia all year round."

"That sounds very good. How much will they pay you?"

"Two hundred florins a year with board and lodging. Not bad to begin with, is it?"

"Not at all, and it might lead to even better opportunities later," said Spangler.

"I must write to my father at once, and to Michael. They'll be as pleased as I am."

48

*Chapter Seven*

HAYDN LIKED his new position with Count Morzin. His duties as conductor and composer were exactly to his taste, and his good disposition helped him get on well with the other musicians. He had to compose music for all kinds of special occasions — birthdays of the Countess and the children, wedding anniversaries, name days, dinner parties. This was good practice and developed his ability to write quickly.

Haydn composed his first symphony for a concert at the Count's castle. He played the harpsichord part, conducting by nodding his head, the customary way in the eighteenth century; he would wave in the strings or wind instruments when it was time for them to come in, and indicate whether to play louder or softer. At the end, the applause he heard behind him was beyond anything he imagined for a composition of his, and he was greatly encouraged.

Among the Count's guests who heard the symphony was Prince Paul Esterházy, whose palace and private orchestra in Hungary were famous. He was so impressed by Haydn's compositions and musicianship that he told his friend Morzin, "Your conductor is a first-rate musician. I shouldn't mind having him myself."

Now that Haydn had a little extra money in his pocket, he began thinking of marriage. Among his pupils in Vienna had been the two daughters of Johann Keller, a hairdresser. Haydn had fallen in love with the younger one, Therese, but she had decided to become a nun. Haydn was deeply disappointed at her decision. Until now, her father had never looked upon him favorably as a suitor anyway; but now that Keller saw that the young man was beginning to earn some money, he urged him to visit them whenever he came to Vienna with the Count. Therese's older sister, who was already thirty-one, three years older than Haydn, seemed likely to be left on her father's hands; and he hoped that since her sister was no longer available, she would win Haydn's affection. The hairdresser's hopes were fulfilled.

It never occurred to Haydn that Maria Anna would be an unsuitable wife. But soon after their marriage he discovered she did not care for music, and she was also jealous and quarrelsome. She made it very plain that it was all one to her whether her husband was an artist or a cobbler.

Worse still, she was unable to have any children. What a terrible disappointment to Haydn! Everything he had wanted of marriage, a peaceful home and a house full of children, was not to be. He threw all his energies into playing, conducting, and composing. And sometimes into pranks.

Once when Haydn and a friend, a talented young musician named Dittersdorf, were roaming the streets of Vienna talking about music, they heard a group of fiddlers scraping out one of Haydn's minuets in a tavern. They went in, and Haydn asked belligerently, "Who composed that music?"

"Joseph Haydn."

"Well, that's a perfectly filthy minuet!" said the composer ferociously.

The fiddlers fell upon him at the insult, but Dittersdorf, who was taller than Haydn, shielded him with his arm until he had pushed him safely outside.

After they had caught their breath, they burst out laughing.

Not long after Haydn's marriage, Count Morzin fell into such serious financial difficulties that he called his conductors and musicians together and told them, "I am sorry to tell you I can no longer afford the luxury of keeping an orchestra. I regret it very much, but you will all have to go."

Haydn's dismissal, added to the disappointment in his wife, seemed almost more than he could bear. Now he would have to begin all over again, trying to find pupils and picking up musical jobs wherever he could.

But no sooner did Prince Esterházy hear of Morzin's financial troubles than he immediately thought of Haydn — the very man he needed for his orchestra at Eisenstadt. If only no one else snapped him up before he got in touch with him!

The Prince still had his old conductor, Gregorius Werner, now old and failing, who had been in his employ for over thirty years. So he offered Haydn the position of assistant conductor for a period of three years. The salary would be four hundred florins a year.

"What luck!" Haydn told Maria Anna. "I will certainly accept the offer."

"I should think so," said his wife. "Why, the pay is twice what Count Morzin gave you, and Prince Esterházy must be greater than some independent princes."

"Yes indeed. The Esterházys have been the greatest landowners in Hungary for years and years. The richest, too. They own sixty market towns and four hundred and fourteen villages in Hungary alone, as well as vast estates in Lower Austria and in Bavaria. I was asking about them today. They are the cream of the Hungarian nobility, and

52

they have had a great reputation for being patrons of art and music. The Prince is himself a capable violinist and cellist."

"Well, I only hope we shall have a decent place to live in," said Maria Anna sourly.

"I must tell you that usually wives are not permitted to come to Eistenstadt with their husbands," said Haydn. "Married quarters are allowed only for the conductor, the first violinist, and sometimes the leading male singers. Let's see what the contract says."

The Prince's contract was long and detailed, clearly setting forth the terms and conditions of Haydn's position at Eisenstadt. It said he would be assistant conductor of the choir, receiving his instructions from the conductor, Gregorius Werner. However, when conducting the orchestra at rehearsals and at performances, Haydn would be his own master.

"Good enough," remarked Haydn, and continued to read aloud. "The contract says I shall be treated as a member of the household and I must behave like an honorable official of a princely household and not drink enough to get drunk and not be overbearing with the musicians, but straightforward and in complete control."

"Naturally!" said Maria Anna, listening carefully.

"When the orchestra is summoned to perform before company, the musicians and I are to appear in the Prince's blue, golden-braided uniforms, white stockings, white linen, and powdered wigs."

"Handsome!" Maria Anna giggled.

"Furthermore, I must not be over-familiar with the musicians or vulgar in eating, drinking, and conversation, lest I lose respect of the men; I must always be a good example, and I must keep the men from being unfriendly or quarreling with one another. That may be difficult.

"With respect to composing, I am to write such music as the Prince commands, and not permit these compositions to be copied; they are to be for the exclusive use of the Prince. I may not compose for anyone else without the Prince's permission."

Haydn stopped, and Maria Anna asked, "What else?"

"Each day I am to appear in the Prince's antechamber before and after midday and inquire whether he wishes the orchestra to perform. Then I pass his orders on to the musicians. I must make sure the musicians are punctual and report those who are late or absent. If unimportant quarrels or complaints arise among the musicians, I must do my best to settle them without disturbing the Prince; but if they are serious, then the Prince should be asked to decide.

"Also I am to take charge of all the music and musical instruments and to be held responsible for any damage to them caused by carelessness or neglect. I am to teach the female singers so that they may not forget in the country what they have been taught in Vienna. I must also practice on all the musical instruments I play, so that I don't lose my skill either. I am glad that is in the contract."

"The Prince certainly intends to get his money's worth," sniffed Maria Anna.

"The orchestra must be developed in such a way that it will bring honor not only to the Prince, but to me, Haydn. The Prince expects me to make improvements, you see. The yearly salary of four hundred florins will be paid in four quarterly payments.

"It doesn't say anything about lodging. I am to board at the officers' table or receive a half gulden a day if I do not.

"This agreement will hold for three years, beginning May 1, 1761; if I decide to leave at the end of that period, I must give the Prince six months' notice. If the Prince is satisfied with me, I may look forward to being appointed conductor; if he isn't, he can dismiss me at the end of the three years."

Maria Anna watched her husband take a quill pen and sign the carefully written document.

"What a contract!" She laughed sourly. "It ties you up body and soul."

"It's absolutely clear and fair, my dear. I know I shall have a lot to do, but I'll enjoy it, every bit of it. Now let me see," said Haydn, counting on his fingers: "I have to practice every day with the orchestra and singers; I conduct the performances and perform a certain amount myself; then I compose much of the music that is to be performed; I have charge of the men, supervise the instruments and music, and keep up my playing on the violin, viola, and harpsichord well enough to perform solos. Many duties, but all very pleasant and just what I like."

"You won't have much time to think of me," said his wife.

"Oh, yes, I will," Haydn assured her; but he did not tell her *how* he would think of her, nor did she know that he had composed a song to a poem by the poet Lessing that said:

> "If in the whole wide world
> But one mean wife there is,
> How sad that each of us
> Should think that one is his!"

*Chapter Eight*

THE MUSICIANS in the Prince's
orchestra were so fond of their new conductor that they began
calling him "Papa Haydn." Not because he was old, for he
was not, but because they appreciated his kindliness and knew
he valued them as people, as well as musicians.

The first time Haydn heard them call him "Papa" he
was touched and pleased. It was nice to know they felt so
warmly toward him. The old conductor, Gregorius Werner,
had never been called by such an affectionate name. Haydn
could see Werner's displeasure at his assistant conductor's
popularity with the musicians.

Nevertheless, Haydn did everything possible to show
his respect and deference for the older man. He consulted

him about programs, about the choice of musicians to play certain compositions, about rehearsals. The fact that Werner could not see the value of Haydn's compositions did not keep Haydn from seeing the value of Werner's; and Haydn showed his respect for Werner not only when Werner was conductor and he was assistant conductor but after Werner was dead and he was conductor.

Werner would not have been sorry to see the men take advantage of Haydn's good nature and friendliness; but Haydn was not called "Papa Haydn" only for his good nature and friendliness. It was apparent that he did not let his warm relationship with the musicians stand in the way of the high standards he set for them. He always required strict attention, good practicing, and beautiful performance. He knew how to bring out the very best in the musicians.

They were devoted to him, and they knew that if they got into trouble with the Prince over some infringement of the rules, Haydn would find ways to help them. The Prince had often punished musicians who did not attend or were late for rehearsals. They might be fined, suspended, or even dismissed.

Both Haydn and Prince Paul were eager to improve the performance of music at the Esterházy palace. Haydn was succeeding so well that he was often able to persuade the Prince to give him his own way about the musicians even when the Prince had intended to assert his authority.

58

One day when the Prince found his assistant conductor copying out parts from his compositions for the men to play he commented, "Well, Haydn, I see you are trying to save me money by doing all the copying yourself. That is very nice of you, to be sure; still, there are some things about which you are far from economical."

"What are you referring to, Your Excellency?" asked Haydn, unabashed.

"You are a little too eager to increase the size of my orchestra. We have twelve musicians, they are all excellent, and I believe them to be sufficient for the operas and concerts to be performed here."

"I am glad you brought the matter up, Your Highness; I was just about to tell you I have found two remarkable young musicians, a violinist and a cellist. I assure you they would improve the quality of our orchestra tremendously."

"Aha, Haydn, just as I thought! And I suppose you need a few more singers to improve the choir?"

"How did you guess, dear Prince?" Haydn smiled. "May I have your permission to engage the talented violinist and cellist?"

"W-e-ll, I can ill afford it, Haydn; but very well, go ahead. As for the additional singers, you can use my servants for now. Some of them have very good voices: I chose them as servants partly for that reason."

"My heartiest thanks, Your Highness. You are very

kind. This will be a splendid opportunity to improve our music, and we will make you even prouder of us."

Haydn was genuinely fond of the music-loving, kindly Prince Paul, with whom he got along so well. It was, therefore, a blow to him when less than a year after his arrival in Eisenstadt, Prince Paul died. What would happen to the musical life there now, Haydn wondered? Since the Prince had no children, his brother, Prince Nicholas, would inherit the estate.

Fortunately the new master turned out to have an even greater passion for music than his brother. He increased Haydn's salary to six hundred florins, though the contract by which he got four hundred florins still had two years to run, and he announced, "I want my court to become a great center of the arts."

Prince Nicholas changed his musicians' uniform to crimson and gold and himself appeared at the court of Maria Theresa in a hussar's uniform covered with jewels. His interest in splendor and show was so great that he became known as "Nicholas the Magnificent." When the musicians laughed about this, Haydn pointed out, "Our Prince is an ideal patron. Despite the way he shows off and loves luxury, he is a kind, generous master and really interested in art and music. He is especially enthusiastic about opera. Already he has asked me to compose five operettas for the festivities to celebrate his inheritance of the estate."

"Is it true that he is going to have a special stage put up in a glass building?"

"Yes, and a French painter will design the scenery."

The next year there were even greater celebrations when the Prince's eldest son was married. They lasted for three days and three nights. For the wedding festivities Haydn composed a pastoral based on the story of Acis and Galatea.

As the festivities for both occasions drew near, Haydn worked hard to have the compositions ready. He stayed up late at night, much to Maria Anna's annoyance, rose early in the morning, copied the parts, rehearsed the orchestra and the singers, supervised the staging, scenery, and lighting, and did his best to keep everyone serene and interested.

At the performances, Haydn sat before his musicians at the harpsichord from which he conducted, dressed in his new crimson and gold uniform, silk stockings, black buckle shoes, ruffle, and white neckcloth, and wearing a white wig, the pigtail tied in back with a ribbon. The music was received with such great praise and enthusiasm that he felt well rewarded for all his labor and effort.

At home in Rohrau, Haydn's father was delighted to hear of his son's success. Matthias told friends, "To think that the son of a village wheelwright should become a famous composer!"

Michael, too, was getting on well. He was concertmaster in the court of the Archbishop of Salzburg and earning a much better salary than he had at Grosswardein. Michael was too far away for visits, but Joseph, at Eisenstadt, was only twenty miles from Rohrau.

In September, 1763, a pile of wood that Matthias used for his work fell on him and he was killed. It had been only a short time since he had come to see his son at Eisenstadt. He had admired Joseph's splendid blue velvet court uniform and enjoyed the music of the well-trained orchestra and the affectionate respect with which the musicians treated their assistant conductor. Prince Nicholas himself had asked Haydn to introduce his father to him so he could tell him how well his son was doing. Haydn was glad that Matthias had lived to see him so well settled in life.

Joseph made over his share of his father's property to his youngest brother, Johann Evangelist. He was only twenty and not very strong — not really up to carrying on his father's wheelwright business. There had been some thought that Joseph or Michael might be able to find Johann Evangelist, or Hansl, as they called him at home, a job as a singer; but his voice was very weak and unimpressive. Finally, however, Joseph was able to get Hansl a place in the Esterházy choir, and whenever he had a spare minute, he gave him singing lessons to develop his voice. Joseph was happy to have this dear member of his family close by, to love and to guide. Hansl lived in the special living quarters for retainers, servants, and musicians on the Esterházy estate, and Joseph looked after him as if he were his cherished child.

Joseph's sisters all married, and he had many nieces and nephews. He took a great interest in them, and when they grew up, in their children, too. Many of them came to live and work in nearby villages, and every year Haydn held a family feast in an inn. He was a wonderful host, and it was a day he looked forward to every year. Maria Anna said he had altogether too many relatives and spent altogether too much money on them; but Haydn loved his relatives and was glad and proud to be able to help them when they needed it or just to do things that would give them pleasure.

Chapter Nine

N 1764 the Archduke Joseph, Maria Theresa's eldest son, was crowned King of the Romans in Frankfort. (This title had very little to do with Rome; it meant he had been chosen to succeed his father as Holy Roman Emperor or presiding officer over a sort of loose union of very independent German rulers and free cities.) Prince Nicholas Esterházy decided to combine his trip to Frankfort for the coronation with a further trip to France and to visit the French royal court at Versailles.

At Versailles the Prince was welcomed by Louis XV as the great nobleman he was. The king showed him the beautiful buildings and gardens at Versailles which had been built by Louis XIV at a cost of over twenty million pounds or a hundred million dollars, adding considerably to the burden of government debt that would eventually drive the overtaxed people of France into revolution.

Prince Nicholas was overcome by the magnificence of Versailles, and, like many a less wealthy prince of the Empire, he was determined to have such a place on his own estate. He noticed and examined everything with the greatest care so he could tell his architect exactly what he wanted.

When he returned, he summoned the architect to a favorite hunting lodge across the Neusiedler See from Eisenstadt. The Neusiedler See was a large lake which overflowed into the surrounding countryside, making a swamp of almost sixteen square miles.

"I wish to have another Versailles," the Prince told his architect, "and will spare nothing to have as beautiful a copy as possible. Come, I'll show you where I want it built. I have thought it all out." With a jeweled hand he pointed out the area where he was planning to build the new palace.

"You don't mean here, Your Excellency, do you?" asked the architect incredulously.

"Exactly! Why not?"

"This swampy land is good only for breeding insects, wild birds, and fever!"

"Nonsense! Clear the swamps, dig canals, and build a dam to hold back the water," commanded the Prince. "Then we can begin the new palace. I'll tell you how many rooms I want and how they should be arranged, so that you can draw up the plans. I have many pictures and accounts of Versailles that I shall want you to study carefully."

"And how many rooms were you thinking of, Your Highness?"

"Well, I think we should have at least one hundred and twenty-five guest rooms, with halls for entertainment and balls. I want several of the rooms done in white marble, and the general effect of the whole should be as splendid as possible. Now, how much do you think such a place is likely to cost, and how long would it take to build?"

After many calculations and many protestations that no estimate could be accurate before plans were even drawn up, the architect said that the new palace and its grounds would cost at least eleven million florins (about five million dollars) and could not be built in less than four years.

The Prince was undaunted. "Let's get on with the work as quickly as possible," he said. "I want my Versailles to be something wonderful to behold."

And so work began. Pumps were installed to dry up the swamps. Some of the water was diverted by canals, some held back by dams. The enormous amount of hard labor to clear the land took many months. Then came the tremendous task of building the new palace. Hundreds of peasants from the surrounding countryside were hired for the work. Craftsmen were brought over from France and Italy.

There were carvers of stone and woodwork, artists to paint scenes on the ceilings and walls, specially trained men to fit together beautiful and intricate inlaid floors.

Eagerly the Prince watched, supervising, making suggestions, criticizing, approving and disapproving. Often he grew impatient and irritable at the time everything was taking, particularly when he saw the expenses mounting into figures the architect had not dared mention.

It took more than four years to fulfill Nicholas's dream completely, but he was able to move his household to the new palace in 1766. When he saw how beautiful his Versailles was, he did not begrudge the huge amounts it had cost him. He was able to make the palace and grounds just as magnificent as he had hoped; and unlike the King of France, he was able to pay for every bit of this splendor.

Haydn, the musicians, and the household staff had been following the progress of the palace and gardens with great interest. It was incredible that anyone could have the amount of money they must have cost. The members of the Esterházy household were almost as proud of their Prince's grandeur as the Prince himself.

One day the Prince took his music director (Werner had died and Haydn had succeeded to his place) on a tour of the new palace. It was even grander and more magnificent than Haydn had imagined! He saw two special rooms for the Prince, containing ten Japanese panels in black lacquer with golden flowers and lovely delicate landscapes painted on them. The remarkable workmanship of the furniture, the rare woods and carvings, made him wish his father could have seen what the foreign craftsmen could do.

The chairs and sofas were covered with handwoven embroidered silks and satins. The clocks in each room played a tune on the hour. Haydn could hear one now, playing a tune that sounded as if it were on a flute. He promised himself that someday he would compose tunes for these ingenious clocks.

The rock crystal chandeliers held hundreds of candles to light the rooms. There were servants whose sole duty it was to tend to the lighting and replacing of candles and to clean the chandeliers in the countless rooms.

There was a library containing valuable editions of rare books and manuscripts and costly engravings. Then there was a special gallery containing works of art by famous Italian and Dutch artists that brought joy to Haydn's heart.

More important to Haydn was the opera house, set apart on the grounds of the huge estate. This was where he would spend a great deal of his time conducting performances of his own operas and those of other composers.

"Your highness, I am overcome with the beauty of the opera house. It looks as if it would hold an audience of at least three hundred people."

"More than that, Haydn, four hundred; and the

boxes on the sides of the theater open into rooms furnished with couches, mirrors, clocks, fireplaces, fine rugs, and mirrors. Come, I'll show you."

Haydn was delighted with everything. "Now, Haydn," the Prince told him, "I wish to have a performance every day at six o'clock, an Italian serious or comic opera or a German comedy. I have made arrangements for special lighting on the stage, and I know the acoustics are good. I shall see to it that you have a good variety of stage settings and the best machinery for special effects. I assure you that the operas you conduct will be seen and heard under the best possible conditions. I am glad to see you are so pleased."

Opposite the opera house was the marionette theater, built like a grotto. Its walls and niches were covered with all kinds of bright-colored stones and shells to give an unusual effect when the candles were lit. The performers would be puppets dressed as richly as human actors and actresses, the voices those of opera singers. There were twelve Italian opera singers in the Esterházy household.

Behind the castle spread the vast park, designed like the one at Versailles, with statues, temples, grottoes, fountains, waterfalls, streams, ponds, bushes trimmed in fanciful shapes, flower beds arranged in intricate designs, imported trees, exotic plants. And beyond was an immense game preserve for hunting.

Haydn could easily appreciate the Prince's elation.

Prince Nicholas, in fact, enjoyed his Versailles so much that he no longer felt the need to go to Vienna in the winter for as long as he had done before. Every year he spent more time in Esterháza. "Everything I need for my enjoyment is right here," he said. "With at least two operas and two concerts a week, plays on other days, chamber music in my apartments, and throngs of noble guests, why should I seek entertainment elsewhere?"

Hearing this, Haydn caught his breath. He knew what his musicians would say. He had already noticed their irritation growing as the Prince kept postponing his departure. The men longed to see their wives and children, who were not allowed to live with them on the Prince's estate. Haydn, as conductor, was an exception.

The large staff of musicians, dancers, singers, painters, copyists, stage designers, puppeteers, and household servants were provided with living quarters in a moderate-sized building on the estate, with strict orders that the men were not to bring their wives, nor the women their husbands, unless they were both engaged for something by the Prince. Those with families in Vienna were given an extra allowance for the expense of keeping them there.

Despite the beauty of their surroundings, the musicians found the climate at Esterháza damp and unhealthy; and an allowance for the support of their families elsewhere was no substitute for the families themselves. When they knew they could go home at regular intervals, they were willing to put up with the separation, but now ——! Haydn very much feared that some of his best musicians might try to find employment elsewhere.

Unfortunately, one attempt to please the Prince had just the opposite effect. One morning when Haydn came for the orders for the day's music, the Prince asked, "By the way, Haydn, have you been composing anything new for me to play on my baryton? I have a great longing to take part in some chamber music soon."

"Yes, Your Excellency, I have. I am also learning to play your favorite instrument myself in order to understand its capacities better. It is by no means easy to play, as I have found out; but I do think it is capable of more than we expected of it. My wife is none too pleased to have me come home late at night and begin practicing on it, but naturally I have no other free time. One thing I discovered is that the baryton can be played in a much wider range of keys than I had thought possible. Perhaps you will permit me to come and play for you and show you how proficient I am becoming on your instrument?"

In an icy tone, the Prince said, "After all, it is your job to know how to play many instruments." He was evidently displeased, and Haydn realized that a display of professional competence on the Prince's own instrument would not be well received. It would be wise to wait awhile before raising the question of the musicians' grievances.

The baryton was an unusual stringed instrument, a member of the viol family with extra complications. Like other viols, it was a fretted stringed instrument played between the knees with a bow. It was a little smaller than a cello, with six or seven gut strings and about twice as many thin wire strings underneath the top ones. They were called sympathetic strings because they resounded when the strings above them were played with the bow. They stretched behind the neck of the instrument and could be plucked (called pizzicato) with the thumb of the left hand, so that with pizzicato and bowing going on simultaneously, the baryton sounded like a viol da gamba and a harp at the same time. The baryton compositions were intended only for private performances, as the tone was small and sounded best in a small room.

Whenever Haydn came from an interview with the Prince, the musicians pressed round him and asked, *"When did the Prince say we could go home?"*

"He did not say, alas. I know how unhappy you must be away from your families for so long, but I'll do my best to find a diplomatic way of getting the Prince to allow you to go home. Just be patient, dear children."

"We rely on you, Papa Haydn," they said gloomily.

Haydn spent several hours thinking of a way to approach the Prince, who would certainly be expecting the

musicians to present their yearly grievance and would be prepared with one of his firm though gracious refusals. How,
Haydn wondered, could he win the Prince's sympathy for
the musicians?

At last he thought of something. He would compose
a new symphony and write it in such a way that its meaning
would be clearer than words. He worked on the composition
with great speed and rehearsed it with the musicians. One
day he told the Prince, "Your Excellency, we have a surprise
for you. A new composition. Will you kindly set a time
when you can hear it?"

Haydn had told each musician beforehand exactly
what he was to do when he finished playing his part in the
last movement. What was the Prince's astonishment to see
the cellist, then the violists, then the violinists, then the wind
players blow out the candles on their music stands as they
finished their parts and solemnly leave the stage. Haydn
alone was left.

At first the Prince was puzzled; then he laughed.
"Aha, Haydn, I see the point perfectly. The musicians wish
to go to their families. Very well, tell them they can pack up
tomorrow and go. It was selfish of me not to think about
it myself. My apologies!"

The symphony, which was Haydn's forty-fifth, became
known as the "Farewell Symphony."

In the three-room apartment provided for Haydn,

Maria Anna waited for him, always ready to complain about something the minute she saw him enter the door. When he saw her scowling face he wished with all his heart he could have had a wife he longed to get back to, or that circumstances had forced him to leave his wife in Vienna.

One day the following summer Haydn came home with news that he thought would interest even Maria Anna. "What do you think, my dear? The Empress Maria Theresa and her retinue are coming to spend several days at Esterháza, and the Prince has asked me to perform my comic opera for her. Isn't that nice?"

Maria Anna shrugged her shoulders, indifferent, and said, "I suppose so." She shuffled into the kitchen to feed the cats while Haydn whistled to the canary. He was thankful God had made him a cheerful, good-natured person. It made life easier.

Haydn was tremendously excited about conducting his comic opera *L'Infedeltá Delusa* before the Empress, and he wanted it to go especially well. It was in two acts and was considered his greatest stage work. The plot concerned a father and two couples who, after many difficulties were suitably matched in a happy ending. The music was delightful and showed that Haydn was now a fully mature composer.

Finally the day of the Empress's arrival came. It was September 1, 1773. Haydn saw her and her attendants approaching in fifteen of Prince Nicholas's magnificently decorated carriages, the coachmen and lackeys in vivid gold-braided uniforms.

In front of the gates kettledrummers and trumpeters standing on a platform broke into a great fanfare. At the doors stood the grenadiers of the Prince's guard in dress uniform; and the whole household was marshaled to do their Queen and Empress honor: servants in their most ornate livery; couriers; lackeys in Hungarian costume; the musicians and their conductor, Haydn; the pack of hounds with their keepers; all the household officials; and six Hungarian pages.

The Prince and his wife received their royal guest at the palace door, surrounded by members of the nobility of Austria and Hungary. After a short rest in the royal apartments, richly decorated for the occasion, the noble guests went to the theater on the grounds of the estate for *L'Infedeltá Delusa*, which was a great success. When it was over, they found the park and the buildings illuminated with lanterns and flares, and everyone gathering for a sumptuous feast outdoors.

Next morning there was an open-air concert under the Empress's windows; then she was taken on a tour of Esterháza to see its beauties and treasures. In the evening a new opera by Haydn was performed, after which he was acclaimed by the entire audience. Another feast followed this, with a masquerade afterwards. One evening there was a marionette opera, the next day there was a hunting party. And so the festivities continued day after day, Haydn providing the music. Afterwards the Empress said, "If I want to enjoy a good opera, I go to Esterháza."

Haydn and his musicians, dressed in their best crimson uniforms, gave a whole program of his latest compositions. Nicholas was glad to show off his remarkable court composer and conductor. The Symphony No. 48, called the "Maria Theresa Symphony" in honor of the Empress, was performed and enthusiastically applauded. At the banquet the next day the best musicians played solos on their instruments. This too added to the prestige of the Prince, for the excellence of his musicians was considered evidence of his taste, musical judgment, and knowledge.

At the marionette theater the Empress attended Haydn's opera, *Philemon and Baucis,* the songs and dialogue sung and spoken by the opera singers behind the scenes. So well did the motion of the puppets synchronize with the voice and tone of the singers that after the eye had grown accustomed to them for a few minutes, it was difficult to remember that they were puppets and not real people. Haydn loved the puppet theater and had a little one of his own. His love of humor could express itself in the lighter puppet operas; the words as well as the music could be more impish when the actors were only puppets.

This particular puppet opera so delighted the Empress that a few years later she asked the Prince if she could borrow the puppets, the scenery, and the musicians for special festivities at her palace in Vienna.

On another day during Maria Theresa's visit to Esterháza, there was a feast with an exciting display of fireworks in her honor. After this the Prince had still another surprise for her. He took her and the other guests to a great open space in the park, illuminated by torches and colored lanterns. Suddenly there appeared almost two thousand peasants in their bright-colored Hungarian and Croatian costumes. To the accompaniment of their own folk music they burst into their national dances and delighted everyone with their exuberance and picturesque appearance.

The next day, before leaving, the Empress gave costly gifts to the people who had helped make her visit such a success, including the music director who had composed, arranged, and conducted the musical events. As she handed Haydn a gold snuff box and graciously thanked him for the pleasure he had given her, he thought with amusement of the occasion at Schönbrunn when she had caught him climbing the scaffolding.

Chapter Ten

HE PRINCE'S frequent guests
and his own demands for entertainment kept his retainers
extremely busy. Despite their good wages and the pleasure
of playing under Haydn, the musicians often grew disgruntled if the Prince did not return to Vienna early in the
autumn. He went there only once in the winter of 1773,
taking his musicians to perform Haydn's compositions for
the benefit of a charitable organization which helped poor
musicians and their families.

This was the first time the Viennese public took any
notice of Haydn's talent. They had considered him a "for-
eigner" because he had been buried at Esterháza for so many
years. There were music critics in Vienna who were not

well-disposed toward Haydn, perhaps because they were envious of his position with Prince Nicholas. They spoke disparagingly about the mixture of the comic and serious in his music and declared he knew little about the rules of music because he was self-taught and had never studied with a great teacher.

When Haydn heard this and saw the intrigues to prevent his music from being performed, he was deeply hurt. Rising to his own defense, he described the musical advantages of his job. "My Prince has always been satisfied with my works and constantly gives me his encouragement and approval. Fortunately, as conductor of his splendid orchestra I can experiment and hear whether what I have composed produces the effect I wish. If it does not please me, I am able to change, add or omit, or be as bold as I like. It is true that I am cut off from the world by being at Esterháza, but that is even an advantage; being isolated as I am, there is no one to confuse or torment me, and I am forced to become original. Never for a moment am I unaware of my good fortune in being in the employ of my music-loving Prince."

He had the opportunity to explore and experiment with the Prince's orchestra to his heart's content. He could try out new effects, blending and contrasting the wind instruments with the strings, solo instruments with full orchestra, experimenting with adventurous harmonies.

Haydn's full orchestra was between sixteen and

twenty-four instruments. At one time he had six violins and violas, one cello, one double bass, one flute, two oboes, two bassoons, and four horns. Later he persuaded the Prince to enlarge the orchestra to twenty-two and twenty-four instruments, including trumpets and kettledrums for special occasions. He also had a group of carefully chosen singers.

Haydn was constantly writing symphonies, music for special occasions like divertimenti (amusement pieces) to help digestion during and after supper, church music, harpsichord and piano pieces, many beautiful quartets and other chamber music, besides operas and other vocal music. The good prince was very appreciative and gave him a free hand.

In his marvelous music Haydn breathed his love of life and sometimes his lively sense of humor. He often used the boisterous songs and dances he had heard as a child in his little village and elsewhere. His music was full of radiance and healthiness, just as Mozart's was full of grace and charm. The Emperor Joseph once said, "I have drawn a parallel between Mozart and Haydn. Mozart's compositions are like a golden snuff box made in Paris and Haydn's like one made in London. Both are beautiful, the former for its adornments, the latter for its simplicity and finish."

Haydn appreciated his position with the Prince even more when he heard that his brother, Michael, who had shown such great talent as a boy and young man, was not fulfilling his early promise as completely as everyone had expected. He was now chapel director and choirmaster for the Archbishop of Salzburg, an irritating and unsatisfactory employer, not only for Michael but also for Leopold Mozart and his son Wolfgang. All the Archbishop's musicians chafed under him.

Michael wrote to Joseph, "The Archbishop here is not as interested in music nor as generous in his salary as your Prince. If I had had as encouraging a hand as was lent you, dear brother, I do not think I should have fallen far behind you."

Joseph agreed that he had been very fortunate. "The daily requirements of my Prince, the lack of diversion and distractions in Esterháza are in many ways a boon to me," he wrote. "Even though I am isolated from the great center of music in Vienna, I manage to keep well informed of what is going on elsewhere, not only in music, but in literature as well.

"Because my home life is what it is I pour my warm feelings into my beloved music; my yearning for children is partially fulfilled by my fondness for the men in my orchestra, who call me 'Papa Haydn.' How sad it is not to have children of my own! I wish you could come here and celebrate with me my forty-seventh birthday. It is hard to believe that I have already been in the employ of the Esterházy family now for eighteen years. How time runs on!"

Haydn did not mention his concern over the rumors that came to him from Salzburg that Michael was drinking too much wine, and that there were times when he could hardly carry out his assignments or compose the works required by the Archbishop. This was a serious matter and disturbed Haydn. He learned that once the young Wolfgang Mozart, who was also in the Archbishop's orchestra, had had to write a composition for Michael and let him hand it in as his own lest he be dismissed.

The year Haydn was forty-seven, a new Italian violinist joined the orchestra. He had a nineteen-year-old wife, who sang in Haydn's operas, and a little son. Among Haydn's many duties at Esterháza was that of teaching and coaching singers for their parts in the opera. Luigia Polzelli thus became one of his pupils. He found her an attractive and charming person and was sorry for her worries about her husband, who was not well. Haydn enjoyed preparing her for the parts she was to perform and took great delight in her company besides, often spending more time teaching her than was actually necessary. Maria Anna noticed this and grew jealous, particularly because Haydn was so fond of Luigia's child.

Luigia's husband, elderly and ailing, did not prove a good enough musician to satisfy the Prince, nor for that matter was the Prince much impressed by Luigia's singing. Their musicianship was neither especially bad nor especially good, and after they had been on his payroll for a year and a half, the Prince told them they could go.

Luigia appealed to Haydn, who did not need to be asked twice, to intercede for her and Antonio. What would poor Antonio do, at his age and with his bad health; what would become of Luigia and her little boy?

Haydn asked to see the Prince to discuss the matter of the dismissal of the Italian violinist and his wife. Prince Nicholas was astonished at Haydn's eloquence as he pleaded their case. His eyes burned with compassion and sympathy for them, especially for the poor little mother. She could develop into a great artist if she were permitted to stay on and he coached her. He would write many operas in which her voice would be exactly right for the part. She would stimulate his talents, he would develop hers.

The Prince smiled and said, "If it means so much to you, Haydn, to have the Polzellis kept on, I'll give them another contract, this time for ten years."

"Thank you, Your Highness," and Haydn bowed gratefully.

Before long Antonio's name had to be dropped from the list of violinists in the orchestra because he was too ill to continue playing. Nevertheless, the Prince continued to pay him. Luigia continued to sing in the operas and to take good care of her sick husband and her children. She had two little boys now, and Haydn loved to play with them. The presence of Luigia and her little ones was such a delight that it gave him new inspiration for his compositions, which became more beautful than ever.

He could hardly wait for her little boys to grow older so he could give them music lessons. If they showed musical talent, how proud he would be! He was as interested in the children and as attentive to them as if they were his own, and he lavished money on them and their young mother.

In addition to Luigia there was another new happiness in Haydn's life. On the occasional trips to Vienna which he made with the Prince, he had at last met the young Wolfgang Mozart, who had left the employ of the Archbishop of Salzburg. The admiration and affection Haydn and Mozart felt for each other was so striking that everyone marveled at the friendship between two people so different in age. Mozart was twenty-five, Haydn forty-nine, when they became friends; but they had so much in common that they were as fast friends as if they were the same age. Haydn was as glad to learn from Mozart as Mozart was to learn from him. They were delighted with each other's music, and they enjoyed each other's company. In their different ways they both had a sense of fun, both in music and in ordinary life, and they naturally had a great many interests in common.

Of course in many ways they were quite different. During one of their talks together Haydn remarked, "What a different musical development yours has been from mine,

Mozart! You began your music almost as a baby and developed with great speed, whereas my progress was slow. At the age you are now, I had not yet composed anything worth mentioning."

"We are quite different in our temperaments," said Mozart. "You have a sweet steady nature and a serene spirit that I envy. There is something else that I envy in you: your good understanding of the value of money. I have absolutely no savings for emergencies. Of course I have no regular patron. I am fortunate when I can give a concert or get a commission to compose an opera, a symphony, or quartet. It is not a life that makes it easy to keep track of one's money, but I seem to be hopelessly irresponsible. Everyone tells me so. You, it is true, have a steady job; but you also seem to be able to get a fair return for your published music, which I never can."

"Yes, I think I am a good match for my publishers. I see to it that I get my fair share, and I intend to save up a tidy sum for my old age. People say I am a precise person; it is true, and I like to be regular in my habits."

Haydn was forced to be a shrewd business man. Music publishing on a large scale was a new trade in Central Europe. Before this, music of all kinds was circulated in manuscript copies. Many music-copying firms thrived in Vienna until the end of the eighteenth century.

Composers received nothing for music distributed by

copyists, who often bribed members of the orchestra to get Haydn's and Mozart's newest works. It was musical piracy; but there was no copyright law, and composers were helpless against the thieving copyists.

Haydn's attitude toward his music publishers was "every man for himself." For years he had watched a large quantity of music published and sold under his name in Paris, London, Berlin, and Amsterdam for which he received nothing. Now he sold his compositions before they could be stolen from him; and it must be admitted that he sometimes sold them twice, though not twice in the same country. A published piece of music was particularly exposed to piracy in another country if regular publication was not arranged for at once. Mozart's concert tours abroad had given him many more musical connections than Haydn, but he was much less able to make financial use of them.

Friends in Vienna often saw Haydn and Mozart strolling together, talking animatedly, two rather short men, Haydn taller and stouter than his friend. Haydn's calm eyes and his long kindly face showed that he meant well by everyone; Mozart's sparkling wit sometimes had a sharp edge to it, but his gaiety was infectious when he was in high spirits. When they were not discussing music, the two musicians were laughing heartily over some joke. There was no rivalry between them. One seemed to supply something the other lacked. They tried out their new works on each other, encouraging each other and learning together.

Was it any wonder, then, that when Prince Nicholas came to Vienna with his musicians, Haydn would take the first opportunity to dash over to see Mozart? After their first affectionate embrace and the excitement of meeting, they would say, "Let's play chamber music with some of our friends tonight."

In February, 1785, when Mozart's father came from Salzburg to see his son, he was present when Mozart, Haydn, and two noblemen, brothers, who were accomplished musicians, performed Mozart's new string quartets together. Afterwards Haydn took Leopold Mozart to one side and said, "I tell you before God, as an honest man, that your son is the greatest composer known to me either in person or by reputation. He has taste, and what is more, the most profound knowledge of composition."

Such praise of Wolfgang from Haydn made Leopold Mozart very proud and happy. He said, "My son insists, dear Haydn, that he learned to write string quartets from you."

"On the contrary, it is I who learn from him!" declared Haydn with deep sincerity. "I cannot understand how one of humanity's benefactors, the most highly gifted musician alive, has not succeeded in finding the patronage he deserves."

"Alas, the intrigues of Viennese musicians against him make things difficult," said the father sadly. "It is a pity."

*Chapter Eleven*

WHEN MOZART published six of his quartets in 1785, he dedicated them "to my dear friend, Haydn," with the following words: "A father, having resolved to send forth his children into the wide world is anxious to entrust them to the protection and guidance of a man who enjoys much celebrity there and who is fortunately his best friend. Here, then, are the children I entrust to a man so renowned and so dear to me . . . During your last stay in Vienna, you yourself, my dearest friend, expressed your satisfaction with them. Be pleased, then, to receive them kindly and be to them a father, a guide and a friend . . ."

Mozart would not permit the least disparaging remark about Haydn in his presence. To one musician who criticized one of Haydn's compositions he said, "I tell you, Sir, that even if they melted you and me together there would still not be stuff enough to make a Haydn."

Haydn, however, declared, when he heard people criticizing various passages in Mozart's opera, *Don Giovanni,* "I cannot settle this dispute, but this I know. Mozart is the greatest composer that the world now possesses." Once when he heard someone express surprise at what he considered Mozart's disregard for the rules of harmony in a string quartet, Haydn said, "If Mozart wrote it, he must have had good reasons for it."

After hearing Mozart's beautiful operas, *The Marriage of Figaro, Cosi Fan Tutti,* and *Don Giovanni,* Haydn grew more and more dissatisfied with his own operas, so that when a letter came to him from Prague in December, 1787, asking him for an opera, he answered, "You wish me to write a comic opera for you. Most willingly if you desire a vocal composition of mine for yourself alone; but if it is with the idea of producing it on the stage at Prague, I cannot comply with your wish, all my operas being too closely connected with our personal circle at Prince Esterházy's in Hungary, so that they could never produce the proper effect, which I have calculated in accordance with the locality. It would be different if I had the invaluable privilege of composing a new opera for your theater. But even then I should be taking a great risk, for scarcely any man could stand comparison with the great Mozart.

"Oh, if only I could explain to every friend of music and especially to the leading men, the inimitable art of Mozart, its depth, the greatness of its emotion, and its unique musical conception, as I myself feel and understand it; nations would then vie with each other to possess so great a jewel within their frontiers. Prague ought to snatch up this precious man — but also to remunerate him; for without this support the history of any great genius is melancholy and gives very little encouragement to posterity to strive more nobly; and for lack of this support many promising talents are lost to the world. It enrages me to think that the unparalleled Mozart had not yet been engaged by some imperial or royal court. Do forgive this outburst — but I love that man too much."

Haydn tried to convince everyone of his friend's greatness, especially since, without a patron, he feared for Mozart a poverty-stricken future. Haydn was not too proud at the age of fifty to tell people how much he had learned from Mozart, while Mozart eagerly acknowledged his own debt to Haydn. Each tried to outdo the other in admitting their musical indebtedness to one another.

Haydn's tributes to Mozart meant a good deal, for his fame had been spreading in spite of his retired life at Esterháza. The King of Spain sent him a gold snuff box set in diamonds in thanks for a composition the Canon of Cadiz had ordered for a service at Cadiz Cathedral. This composition, *The Seven Last Words of our Saviour on the Cross,* turned out to be one of Haydn's finest works.

In addition to the King of Spain's gift, Haydn received another small box in payment from the Canon of Cadiz. He opened it expectantly and found only a small chocolate cake. This was a disappointment, but being a good-natured and generous person, Haydn decided to share the cake with friends and enjoy it anyway.

When he cut into it, his knife hit something hard. He tried another part of the cake, but somehow the knife kept hitting an obstacle. It simply would not cut through to the bottom. Haydn decided to take a good look inside the cake; to his amazement and delight he discovered fifty gold pieces!

*The Seven Last Words* was successful outside of Cadiz and became very well known. In 1793, when George Washington was President, a performance of this composition was given in the United States.

More and more requests for Haydn's compositions were coming in, and Prince Nicholas was generous enough not to attempt to monopolize his music director's writings. After all, Haydn's growing fame contributed to his own reputation as a magnificent patron of the arts. In 1784 a French concert society commissioned Haydn to write six symphonies for them. They were to be performed in Paris with some of his other compositions. In London it was Haydn's string quartets which became especially popular.

The Prince of Wales, who was a cellist, delighted in playing them with friends.

Music was fashionable in London. The Royal Family were keen amateurs and performers of music. There were music societies and clubs of all kinds which rivaled each other in the quality of their concerts. Operas and concerts were supported not only by the nobility but by the well-to-do middle class.

Consequently there were now letters from English publishers offering Haydn large sums if he would let them have his compositions. One publisher, John Bland, came to Esterháza in hopes of obtaining from Haydn not only new compositions but a promise to come to England to give concerts. He did not get that, but during his visit, he happened to be in the room when Haydn was shaving and having trouble with a dull razor. "I would give my best quartet for a good razor!" Haydn exclaimed. Hearing this, Mr. Bland rushed to his room and breathlessly returned with a fine set of English razors.

"Now, Mr. Haydn, where is the quartet?"

Amused at the way he had been caught, Haydn gladly gave the Englishman his string quartet, Opus 55, No. 2, which became known as the "Razor Quartet."

Italy was not slow in showing Haydn that he was as greatly appreciated there as he was in France and England. He had become a great favorite among the Italian musicians,

and the Philharmonic Society of Modena honored him by electing him to its membership. The most important music society in Vienna, which Haydn very much wished to join, had refused to make him a member. In Vienna some musicians still chose to regard him as a self-taught amateur.

King Ferdinand IV of Naples, a great music lover though an abominable king, commissioned several concertos for his favorite instrument, the lira organizzata. This was a sort of hurdy-gurdy that looked like a big viola. Inside there was a wooden wheel, turned by a crank, which pressed on the strings from below and set them vibrating. The strings were not shortened with the fingers but with wooden bridges operated by keys or pegs.

A little organ attachment was built into the instrument. The keys that shortened the strings at the same time let air into the tiny pipes, and the wheel that acted as a bow also worked the bellows. Haydn wrote five concertos for this curious instrument, although fast passages were impossible on it and it had a range of only two octaves. The lira concertos were chamber music, music for a small group of instruments. They were written for two violins, two violas, one cello, two horns, and two lire.

The King of Prussia, Frederick Wilhelm II, an excellent cellist, for whom Mozart wrote his last two quartets and to whom Beethoven dedicated two cello sonatas, sent Haydn a diamond ring in appreciation of his compositions.

Still another valuable ring was given to him by the Russian Grand Duchess Maria Fedorovna. When she was visiting Vienna, Haydn had given her music lessons and had written for her such lovely songs that she wished to show her appreciation.

It was customary for composers to send their compositions as presents, with or without dedications, to kings or nobles in order to call themselves to their attention and perhaps win their patronage. Mozart and Beethoven often did this, and Haydn did too, but chiefly to members of the Esterházy family.

Haydn liked the King of Prussia's ring so much that he always put it on when he began composing an important new work, declaring, "It brings me luck." Not relying entirely on the ring, however, he always said a prayer before sitting down to compose. Sometimes if the composing was not going well, he got down on his knees and implored the Lord for help and inspiration. He never failed to write on a completed composition, "Praise be to God."

Because of the growing demand for his compositions from foreign publishers, Haydn was now able to get good sums, and it pleased him to see his savings grow. By the 1780's the Viennese publishers, who had been slow to appreciate Haydn properly, decided they had better not be left behind or all his compositions would go to foreign publishers. Their attitude toward him began to change. They had suddenly discovered that there was an important composer in their midst.

For Haydn this was a victory, and although he would have liked to say, "It was high time that you recognized me!" he remained his simple, kindly self. The main thing that mattered to him was that people enjoy his music. It was a way of serving God in thanks for giving him musical talent and a cheerful nature.

*Chapter Twelve*

THERE WERE many well-edu-
cated and well-off people in Vienna — high officials, nobles,
and prosperous people of the middle class — who enjoyed
concerts of orchestral music in their homes. Some of the
performers were very talented amateurs.

The home that Haydn loved the most was that of
Dr. Peter Genzinger, who was Prince Esterházy's physician.
The doctor and his charming wife, Marianne, an excellent
singer and pianist, were ardent lovers of music. On Sundays
people who shared their taste for music were invited to their
home to hear beautiful performances of compositions by old
and new composers. Whenever Haydn was in Vienna on a
Sunday, he hastened to take part in these musical evenings.

Marianne Genzinger, her children, and her home offered him much that he had missed in his own married life. The deep interest she showed in his compositions, the way she prepared his favorite dishes and consulted him about her children's musical education, made his life ever so much sweeter.

However, after spending a happy Sunday with the Genzingers, he returned to Esterháza feeling lonelier than before. Frequent letters from Marianne cheered him, and his letters to her poured out his feelings to his dear and understanding friend. A long one written on February 9, 1790 (he had left Vienna February 4), began gloomily, "Well, here I sit in my wilderness, lonely, like a poor orphan, almost without human society, melancholy, full of the memory of past glorious days . . . those delightful gatherings where a whole circle is one heart, one soul, all those lovely musical evenings which I can only think about, not write about . . ." He had found everything in confusion and had been very busy, and how he had missed the comforts of Vienna! "Here in Esterháza no one asks me, "Chocolate? With or without milk? Do you need some coffee? Black or with cream? What can I give you, my dear Haydn? Should you like vanilla ice or pineapple?"

After all his years with the Esterházy family, Haydn had finally got bored and even begun looking upon himself as a slave. How much pleasanter it was to live in Vienna where he could have the inspiring companionship of Mozart and the warm friendship of Marianne and her husband! In addition, there were now all kinds of invitations from foreign countries to come and conduct his compositions. He longed to accept them before he was too old to see the world a bit; but since he was in the employ of the Esterházy family, how could he? Although he was almost sixty years old, his vitality and youthful spirits were such that everyone who knew him said he was like a man half his age. He wrote to Marianne, "I need change, new experiences. I wish to be with people who can stimulate and inspire me. My sleeping forces are waiting to be awakened further. But how can I tell the Prince I want to leave after being in the employ of his family for almost thirty years? Well, I will bide my time and see how to regain my release gracefully."

At last fate came to his rescue. In the autumn of 1790 Prince Nicholas died, and his son, Anton, who had never shared his father's interest in music, quickly dismissed all the musicians except Haydn and his best violinist and a few wind players. Haydn grieved for his generous and musical patron, but seized the opportunity to escape. Prince Nicholas had left him a pension of one thousand florins a year, to which Anton added four hundred a year in salary so that Haydn would still remain in the employ of the Esterházy family. But Haydn saw that it really would not matter to the new prince whether he stayed on or not, and he asked for a leave of absence. The moment the Prince consented to his request,

Haydn rushed to Vienna, so eager to get away that he left most of his belongings in Esterháza. Maria Anna remained in their house in the village below the Esterházy castle at Eisenstadt.

In Vienna Haydn moved into an apartment in the house of his friend Nepomuk Hamberger. As soon as his new freedom became known, offers came pouring in from other patrons. But Haydn was in no hurry to accept any of them.

One day a man came to him and introduced himself as Johann Peter Salomon of London, saying, "I have come from London to fetch you." He was a German musician from Bonn who had lived in England for nine years and had made a great success there. Salomon had been an ardent admirer of Haydn's music for a long time — it was he who had sent Mr. Bland, the Englishman who bartered his razors for a quartet, to try to persuade Haydn to come to England three years earlier — and he offered Haydn twelve hundred pounds (then about six thousand dollars) to compose for him a new opera, six symphonies, and twenty smaller compositions and conduct them at concerts in London. "I am willing to deposit five thousand florins with your bankers as a guarantee right now," he said.

"That is a very handsome offer, Mr. Salomon," said Haydn. "I have heard of the large and well-trained orchestras in England, and I know my works are appreciated there. But let me think the matter over for a little while."

Haydn was greatly tempted. This was his chance to compose exactly as he pleased and not have to write music for special occasions or as background for something else as he did at Esterháza. He had an offer from the King of Naples, but that would be court life again, and he was no longer so eager to go to Italy as he had once been. He was less interested in writing operas than he had been; Mozart had the genius for that. There was, however, the difficulty that he knew Italian and did not know English.

Mr. Salomon stayed in Vienna for several days waiting anxiously for Haydn's answer. When, at last, Haydn accepted his terms, Salomon was so overjoyed at the success of his mission that he decided to stay in Vienna until Haydn could go to England with him.

"But, Salomon, do you realize that I don't speak a word of English?"

"Oh, it doesn't matter in the least, my friend. You'll learn enough to get along while you're in London."

When Haydn's Viennese friends heard he was going to England, they told him, "It is dangerous for a man of your age to start out on such a great journey!" They pointed out that England was an island and that he would have to cross the English Channel to get there — he, who had never even seen the sea.

Full of enthusiasm and bouncing energy, Haydn replied, "I am not in the least afraid. I am in excellent health and I have a great curiosity about the world."

Mozart was the most worried of all about Haydn's leaving and implored him not to go, saying, "Best of friends, you have had no education for the wide world and you speak so few languages. It will be a great handicap."

"I need no other language but the language of music, dear Mozart. That language is understood everywhere."

Salomon grew uneasy when he saw how Haydn's friends felt about his going to England. He feared they might dissuade him if they kept on talking about his making the trip; so he hardly let Haydn out of his sight. Fortunately, Haydn liked Salomon and they became very good friends.

At last it was almost time to leave for London. Haydn went to say good-bye to Marianne and her family. As a parting present he gave her a "Farewell Song," the words of which said, "Think of me when sea and land are between us. Now when we have just begun to know each other well, we have to part."

Then he went to see Luigia and her two boys. After that he spent a day with Mozart, the most cherished friend of them all, talking, joking, laughing, making music with him. On the day of Haydn's departure, December 15, 1790, the two friends said farewell to each other with a warm embrace. Haydn saw tears in his friend's eyes; he seemed full of forebodings and said sadly, "Dearest friend Haydn, I fear this will be our last farewell."

Haydn and Salomon traveled through Germany —
stopping off in Bonn, Salomon's birthplace — and crossed
to England from Calais. Haydn wrote to Marianne: ". . . on
New Year's Day, after attending early Mass, I went on
board at seven-thirty in the morning and at five in the afternoon arrived safe and sound at Dover, for which God be
thanked. At first for four whole hours we had hardly any
wind and the ship went so slowly that in those four hours we
made no more than one single English mile. And from
Calais to Dover is twenty-four miles. . . . Happily, around
eleven-thirty such a favorable wind rose that by four o'clock
we had covered twenty-two miles. . . . During the whole
crossing, I stayed on **deck**, so as to gaze my fill at that enormous beast, the ocean.

"So long as it was calm I had no fears. At the last,
however, when the wind broke out, rising every minute, and
I saw the high, impetuous waves dashing against the ship,
I suffered a little fear and also a little seasickness. But I over-
came it all and arrived safely in harbor without being actually
sick. Most of the passengers were sick.

"I did not feel the strain of the journey until I arrived
in London, but I needed two days to recover from it. But now
I am quite fresh and well, and admiring the endless great
city of London, which quite astonishes me with its varied
beauties and wonders."

London was an entirely new world to Haydn, who

had never been outside a small part of Austria and the border of Hungary. It was a much larger and busier city than Vienna. Haydn found it very exciting, but said he wished he could fly back to Vienna for quiet to work in. "The noise of all sorts of pedlars crying their wares in the street is unbearable!"

"You'll get used to it, Haydn," said Salomon. "You certainly have the spirit of a young man and a wonderful curiosity about everything. I am not at all worried about your getting a footing in this new world."

Haydn was interested in everything, especially in everyday details of life. He set down in his diary, "Arrived in London January 1791. London has four thousand carts for cleaning the streets, burns eight hundred thousand cartloads of coal a year. If anybody steals two pounds (ten dollars) he is hanged."

Haydn was delighted to find old acquaintances from Vienna turning up in London. Celebrated musicians came to England to receive honors and the large sums of money offered in order to build London's musical life to new heights. So many concerts were going on that rivalries were growing up betwen various music societies. The London newspapers made a great deal of Haydn's arrival in London; he was considered such an important person that the Austrian and Neapolitan ambassadors promptly returned his duty calls, to pay their respects. It was all very flattering.

*Chapter Thirteen*

IN HIS first letter from London, after only a week there, Haydn wrote to Marianne, "I was invited for dinner six times and I could have been every day if I had wished." He attended many concerts and was greatly impressed by the size and quality of the English orchestras. Eighteen days after his arrival in London, he was invited to a court ball given in honor of the Queen's birthday. The Prince of Wales, the future George IV, covered with diamonds of more than Esterházy splendor, was very polite to Haydn and invited him to make music at his own house.

Before Haydn's concerts were to begin, Salomon's rivals began circulating rumors about him, saying, "Although Haydn is a great composer, he is, after all, an old man whose powers are waning. He is bound to disappoint the high expectations of the friends of music here."

Haydn was offended, but instead of being discouraged, he worked harder with the orchestra that was to perform his works, so as not to disappoint the English public. When the day arrived on which he was to give the first performance, Haydn saw an excited and dazzling audience, the ladies in elaborate hoop skirts and embroidered gowns and high powdered headdresses, the gentlemen in colored suits of rich stuffs and wearing swords by their sides. The soloists appeared on the stage preceded by sword-bearers as a guard of honor. This ceremonious way of beginning the concert served to heighten the expectations of the eager audience.

The concert was magnificent. The climax was Haydn's new symphony in D major, his ninety-third, written for this occasion. Salomon was the concertmaster, leading the violin section, and Haydn conducted from the piano. The more delicate harpsichord was now superseded by the stronger piano, which could be heard better in the larger concert halls with the bigger orchestras.

Haydn's new symphony was a tremendous success. The audience was so enthusiastic that they rose to their feet in excitement. They were especially stirred by the slow movement, which they applauded until it was repeated — an unusual occurrence, because it was usually the slow movements that audiences found boring.

Haydn was so pleased with his success that before he went to bed that night he wrote down everything in his diary so that he wouldn't forget. His position in the musical life of London was established, and the next morning one of the London newspapers said, "We cannot suppress our very anxious hope that the first musical genius of the age may be induced by our liberal welcome to take up residence in England."

The public concerts that followed were just as great a triumph, and because of this, when Haydn gave a benefit concert in May, he received almost twice the amount he had been guaranteed. Haydn was overcome by the response and applause of the huge and enthusiastic audiences. He had never had such vociferous appreciation, and it made him want to compose more works and give the public the best that was in him.

Before coming to London he had performed his works mostly for a small and intimate circle of music lovers and musicians. Now, with a large orchestra and a larger and more diverse public who responded heartily to his music, his musical creativeness was greatly stimulated. The twelve symphonies he wrote for Salomon, the "London Sym-phonies," show much that is new both in form and in spirit. Haydn's gratitude to England was expressed in a bright-ness, a joy and gaiety that makes them the crown of his sixty years.

The Prince of Wales was greatly taken with Haydn as a person as well as a musician, and invited him to Carleton House twenty-six times to make music with him. The bill for these performances was one of the many that this expensive prince did not pay; but later on, upon the advice of his friends, Haydn finally decided to send a bill to Parliament, and that bill was promptly paid. The Prince played the cello not at all badly, and Haydn wrote to Marianne, "The Prince of Wales is the handsomest figure of a man on God's earth, loves music extravagantly, has much feeling, but little money."

A great many people called on Haydn, among them Clementi, an Italian Englishman who was now a piano dealer and music publisher in London. He was an accomplished pianist and composer and had once entered a contest in Vienna with the young Mozart. There were also the Storaces, brother and sister, English singers who had lived in Vienna and taken part in some of Mozart's operas and at whose home Haydn and Mozart had played chamber music. It was pleasant to see all these cordial and friendly people. In the eighteen months Haydn remained in London his circle of friends grew larger and larger, and always by his side was his devoted friend Salomon to help him.

Many of the musicians could speak German or Italian, and Haydn was learning English fast. Members of the royal family could understand German, for George III was

Elector of Hanover as well as King of England, and princes of the Hanover family had been marrying German princesses since they came to the throne of England nearly eighty years before Haydn's visit.

The musicians who played under Haydn were as enthusiastic about him as the English audiences. They found him kind and patient, his explanations clear even in translation, his conducting a source of inspiration. He rehearsed them very carefully and showed them by example just how he wanted difficult passages played. They tried to perform his compositions as beautifully as they could.

At the end of May, Haydn attended a Handel Festival at Westminster Abbey. An Englishman who saw him in the audience wrote, "Haydn was present at the performance and with the aid of a telescope, which had been placed on a stand near the kettledrums, I saw the composer near the king's box." There was a very large audience. "The female fashions of the day were found highly inconvenient, particularly the headdresses, and it was ordered that no caps should be admitted of a larger size than the pattern exhibited at the Lord Chamberlain's office." The demand for hairdressers was so great that many of the ladies had to have their hair dressed and powdered the night before, and in order not to muss their hair they sat up all night to be ready for early admission to the Abbey in the morning.

Haydn was so overcome by the Hallelujah Chorus

of *The Messiah,* and by the respect and reverence with which the audience stood up and listened to Handel's glorious music, that he burst into tears and said, "He is the master of us all!" He was impressed with what could be done with great massed choruses and a large orchestra, and he hoped that some day he might try composing an oratorio. During the summer, while he was at work on compositions for the following season in London, he would often think about it.

In July Haydn was invited to Oxford University to receive the honorary degree of Doctor of Music. During the three days he was at Oxford, three concerts with brilliant soloists were given in his honor, and Haydn was deeply touched by the tribute. When he came out to take his bow in his cherry-colored doctor's gown, the applause was tremendous. Haydn delightedly showed off his gown and called "I thank you" in English. The exhilarating Symphony No. 92, composed some years before, came to be known as the "Oxford Symphony" because it was played in the first Oxford concert when Haydn was there. Later Haydn sent the university a lovely three-part song, "Thy Voice, O Harmony." Haydn told friends, "Singing is almost one of the forgotten arts, and that is why instruments are often allowed to overpower the voice. Composers should all learn to sing."

Haydn loved wearing the Oxford doctor's cap and gown of red and cream-colored silk during his three days in Oxford, and he wrote to Marianne, "I only wish my friends in Vienna could have seen me!" In his diary he jotted down, more prosaically, "I had to pay one-and-a-half guineas for the bell peals at Oxford when I received the Doctor's degree, and half a guinea for [hiring] the gown. The journey cost six guineas."

Afterwards in very formal letters he sometimes put "Doctor at Oxford" after his name. The honor added to his position in Vienna. It showed that his success in England had been more than a mere commercial success.

Haydn traveled about England during the summer, visiting friends and having a wonderful time. He wrote to Marianne in the autumn, "Oh, my dear gracious Lady! How sweet is the taste of a certain liberty! I had a good prince but had to be dependent on base souls at times. I often sighed for release, and now in some measure I have it. . . . The consciousness of no longer being a bond servant sweetens all my toil."

Suddenly Haydn received a letter from Prince Anton telling him that he had been away for a long time and demanding that he return at once to compose an opera for a celebration in honor of the Emperor.

Haydn had to answer that he was under contract with Mr. Salomon for the coming season. Would the Prince be furious with him for not complying with his wish? He wondered. Sorrowfully, he awaited a letter of dismissal; but to his infinite relief, the Prince did not press the matter. Now that Haydn had become such a famous composer, having him in the Esterházy family was worth a good deal in prestige.

When Haydn returned to London, he went to work immediately on the compositions he was preparing for the new season. There were still more dinners and parties to go to, and after one of them he was so interested in the dancing and music that he wrote in his diary, "Nothing but minuets are danced in this room; but I could not stay longer than a quarter of an hour. First, because of the heat caused by so many people being crowded into so small a room; secondly, because of the wretched dance music, two violins and one violoncello composing the whole orchestra. The minuets were more Polish than German or Italian. Then I went into another room that looked more like a subterranean cave. There the dance was English and the music was a little better because there was a drum that drowned the blunders of the fiddlers. I went on to the great hall where we had dined; here the music was more tolerable. The dance was English but only on the elevated platform where the Lord Mayor and the first four members had dined. The other tables were all newly surrounded by men who, as usual, drank right lustily all night long. The most singular thing of all, however, was the fact that a part of the company danced on without hearing a note of the music, for first at one table, then at another, some were howling songs and some drinking toasts amidst the maddest shrieks of Hurrah! Hurrah!"

To Marianne Genzinger he wrote of his visit at a country house where the Duke of York (one of George III's younger sons) was spending his honeymoon with his seventeen-year-old bride, daughter of the cello-playing king who had sent Haydn his diamond ring, Frederick Wilhelm II of Prussia. "She (the young duchess) is the most charming lady in the world, has a very good understanding, plays the piano, and sings very nicely. . . . She stayed beside me from ten in the evening, when the music began, till two hours after midnight. Nothing but Haydn's music was played. The sweet little thing sat beside me on the left hand and hummed all the pieces from memory, because she had so often heard them in Berlin. The Prince of Wales sat at my right and accompanied me on the cello tolerably well. I had to sing, too. . . . On the third day, as I couldn't get a post horse, the Duke of York sent me two stages in his coach."

The Prince of Wales had Haydn's portrait painted for his private sitting room. When, as George IV, he made Buckingham House into Buckingham Palace, it was moved there, where it still is. This portrait, by John Hoppner, shows Haydn as a vigorous man with regular features, a long nose, and thick, dark eyebrows. His complexion was dark, his face pitted by smallpox. His dark grey eyes beamed with benevolence. He said of himself, "Anyone can see by the look of me that I am a good-natured sort of fellow."

Salomon's rivals tried to win over Haydn and induce

him to give concerts for them, but nothing could swerve his loyalty from Salomon. They therefore decided to produce a competitor for Haydn, and this competitor was his former pupil, Ignaz Pleyel. In spite of the much-advertised competition between them, Haydn and his pupil remained excellent friends; they often had dinner together and enjoyed each other's company. Whenever anyone spoke to Haydn about what a great artist Pleyel was, Haydn praised him generously.

There was really no comparison between Pleyel and Haydn, but Salomon's rivals were determined there should be a race between them to see who could compose the most while they were in London. It was at this time that Haydn composed the lovely "Surprise Symphony," No. 94, with the unexpected jolt after a quiet section. The newspapers were most enthusiastic, and Haydn's second benefit concert was very successful. In fact there was so much enthusiasm for Salomon's twelve Haydn concerts that he gave an extra one to finish up with. This made fourteen concerts in one season — Salomon's thirteen and Haydn's benefit concert — programmed mainly of Haydn's compositions and rehearsed and conducted by Haydn. Haydn did some teaching, too, and wrote accompaniments for Scotch songs to help a publisher, a fine musician who was having financial difficulties. These were a great success, and so profitable both to the publisher and to Haydn himself that later Haydn set more Scotch songs and a series of Welsh songs.

Despite the fact that Haydn was in good physical condition and bouncing with exuberance and energy, his active social life in addition to his busy musical one was beginning to exhaust him. Although his creative forces and zestfulness were as great as ever, the damp winter climate of London made his bones ache with what he called the "English rheumatism." In November he had experienced his first London fog and noted in his diary, "There was a fog so thick that I might have spread it on bread. In order to write I had to light a candle at eleven o'clock in the morning." He did not like English food as well as Austrian, and he often thought of the delicious things he had eaten at the home of the kind Genzingers.

Next summer, when the concert season was over, Haydn again explored the English countryside, seeing as much as he could. One day he went to the Ascot races and later wrote in his diary: "In the first heat there were three riders who were compelled to go around the course twice without stopping. They did it in five minutes. No stranger would believe it unless he were convinced by observation. The second time there were seven riders and when they approached some fell back, but never more than about ten paces and when one thinks the one rider who is about to reach the goal will be the first, at which moment large bets are laid on him, another rushes past him with inconceivable force and reaches the winning post. The riders are very lightly clad in silk, each of a different color, to make it easier to recognize them and all lean as greyhounds. The horses are of the finest breeds, light, with very slender legs, the manes plaited into braids, the hoofs very neat. As soon as they hear the sound of the bell they dash off with the greatest force. Every leap of the horses is twenty-two feet long. These horses are very costly. A few years ago the Prince of Wales paid eight thousand pounds for one and sold it again for six thousand. But the first time he won fifty thousand pounds with it."

Now that the concerts and his travels were over, Haydn began getting ready to return to Vienna. He wrote to Marianne, "I am all tired out and exhausted with so much work and am looking forward to a rest." His English friends kept urging him to stay.

"I promise to come back," said Haydn, "but now I must go home and put my affairs in order. Besides, Prince Esterházy has summoned me to Frankfort for the coronation of our new Emperor, Francis II."

He began packing his trunks, putting into them presents for his friends at home. There were English scissors, needles, knives, spectacles, steel chains, and other articles for which England was well known.

Although it had been wonderful to be in England, Haydn was very eager to go home; he could hardly wait to see Vienna and all the good friends he had left there. The many farewell dinners given in his honor were delightful occasions, and Haydn told his English friends and admirers, "My visit to England has been the most exciting time in my life. I thank you for all you have done for me, and I promise to return to you."

The sincerity of his manner, the warmth of his friendship and affection reassured his devoted English friends, so reluctant to see him leave their country. They simply had to have him back.

In his diary he wrote, "God in one's heart, a good little wife in one's arm; the first brings salvation, the second warmth."

But it was not of Maria Anna he was thinking. She had been sending him venomous letters, demanding money to buy a house she had seen which she said would be nice for her to live in when she was a widow!

With his English earnings Haydn would now be able to buy the house she wanted, but as for her confident expectation of becoming a widow, who could tell? He might outlast her!

*Chapter Fourteen*

O N THE way to Vienna, Haydn stopped off again at Bonn, where he had been eighteen months ago with Salomon, before they went to England. The Elector had already left for the coronation in Frankfort, but the members of his orchestra, honored by Haydn's visit to their city and full of admiration for his music, invited him to have breakfast with them at a delightful inn on the Rhine, in the village of Godesberg.

It was here that one of the young musicians, who was to become one of the world's most famous composers, approached Haydn and introduced himself.

"May I have your opinion about my cantata, Dr. Haydn?" asked Ludwig van Beethoven.

"Ah, so you are the Beethoven who came to Vienna as a lad to study with the great Mozart."

"Yes sir. I had to go home suddenly because of my sick mother."

"And then they needed you at home," said Haydn sympathetically, and he began looking over Beethoven's composition. His face lighted up with the pleasure of hearing the music in his head as his eyes scanned the pages.

"It is good, Beethoven. Perhaps one day you will come to Vienna again. If you do, be sure to come and see me. I may be able to help you. I should be very happy to have you as my pupil if you can obtain leave from your Elector to come to Vienna."

Beethoven's serious face became transformed as he heard this invitation from the master whose compositions he admired so much. It was just what he had hoped for. He had not been as happy as this for a long time. Oh, what he could accomplish working under such a teacher as Haydn, away from his household cares! His mother had died long ago and he was both father and mother to his brothers, although his shiftless father was still alive. He would do everything possible to get to Vienna again.

When Haydn left Bonn he went directly to Frankfort, wondering whether his Prince would be very much annoyed with him for staying in England so long. When they met, however, there were no reproaches. "Well, Haydn," remarked the Prince, "I see a change for the better in your dress, manner, and worldliness. I congratulate you."

At last the festivities in Frankfort were finished and Haydn could go on to Vienna, where he longed to be. No fuss was made over his arrival in Vienna, no concerts arranged. It was the dead time of summer, and besides, it was war time. The Austrian army was marching to help the King of France and his beautiful Austrian Queen, a daughter of Maria Theresa's, to put down the rebellious Assembly that had done away with the privileges of the nobility and the clergy and was keeping the Royal Family prisoner. There was not even the smallest notice in the newspapers announcing Haydn's return to Vienna. His old friends, however, took notice enough. They were delighted to see him again.

But the friend he wanted to see the most was missing. Mozart had died while Haydn was in England. Sadly Haydn recalled how Mozart had wept at their last parting, full of foreboding about ever seeing him again.

When Haydn had heard rumors of Mozart's death, he had at first refused to believe them. Afterwards he had written to their mutual friend and fellow-Mason, Puchberg, who had often lent Mozart money to tide him over, "I was for some time quite beside myself over his death and could not believe that Providence should so quickly have called an irreplaceable man into the other world. . . Have the goodness, my dear friend, to send me a list of his works that are not yet known here. I'd like to do what I can to push them for the widow. I wrote to the poor soul myself three weeks ago, telling her that when her dear son is old enough, I will teach him composition myself without payment to the best of my power, so as to take the place of his father in some measure."

To Marianne he had written, "I am looking forward like a child to being at home again and embracing all my old friends; my one grief is that the great Mozart will be missing, if indeed it is true, which I hope it is not. The world will not see a talent like that again in a hundred years!"

Haydn urged English publishers to print Mozart's compositions and told them, "Friends often flatter me that I have some genius, but Mozart stood far above me."

Once, fifteen years after Mozart's death, when his name was mentioned, Haydn, then an old man, burst into tears and said, "Forgive me. I must ever, ever weep when I hear the name of my Mozart."

Haydn turned to Marianne Genzinger for comfort. She had always been interested in his compositions and in his welfare. He went to her home as if it were his own, played her his new compositions, told her about England, enjoyed her children. Life did not seem so dreary in his own home with Maria Anna, so long as he could see these fine, warm-hearted people.

But now a new blow fell. Within a year of Haydn's return to Vienna, Marianne Genzinger died. She was a young woman, only thirty-eight, and left five children. The shock of her death suddenly changed Haydn's amiable attitude toward the world to impatience and bitterness. Each day he felt his loss more keenly. Mozart gone — Marianne gone!

Fortunately there were several new and talented pupils to distract him from his melancholy thoughts; among them was the young Beethoven, who had brought with him a friendship album in which was a farewell letter from his good friend in Bonn, Count Waldstein, which said: "Dear Beethoven: You are traveling to Vienna in fulfillment of your long cherished wish. . . . Labor assiduously and receive Mozart's spirit from the hands of Haydn."

Haydn was pleased that Beethoven had come to study with him, and he wanted to help him, to be his good friend. Knowing how little money Beethoven had, Haydn charged him almost nothing for the lessons in composition. Haydn soon found, however, that the young chap from Bonn was rather ill-tempered, suspicious, his ideas strong and fixed. One had to know how to get on with him. In fact he was as stubborn as a mule!

Not wishing to quarrel with him, Haydn thought the best way to get along with him was to tease him good-naturedly, so he began calling him "The Grand Mogul"; he had all the fierce pride of an Oriental potentate.

Haydn did not know that Beethoven was disappointed in him as a teacher. The young man told a friend, "Haydn is a fine composer and a good person, but he overlooks mistakes. He is so absorbed in his own thoughts and new compositions that he hates to bother correcting elementary exercises. I can't blame him, but after all, I came to Vienna to learn something. What I need is a stricter teacher. I'll have to go secretly to someone else — without telling him, for I would not hurt his feelings for the world."

Some time later when Beethoven composed some piano sonatas he dedicated them to Haydn, who praised them highly. He was more cautious in his praise of two trios which Beethoven also dedicated to him, telling the young composer, "I advise you not to publish the Trio in C Minor until you have made a name for yourself."

"And why not?" asked Beethoven suspiciously.

"Because it is too revolutionary and it won't be appreciated properly."

The advice was given in good faith and based on ripe experience, but Beethoven was angry and decided that Haydn was jealous of his composition.

He did not know that Haydn had written to his Elector, the Archbishop of Cologne:

"Vienna, the 23rd of November, 1793

"Your Electoral Grace:

"I take the liberty of sending your Electoral Grace some musical works, a quintet, an eight-voice partita, an oboe concerto, variations for the pianoforte, and a fugue, compositions of my dear pupil Beethoven with whose care I have been graciously entrusted. I flatter myself that these pieces, which I may recommend as evidence of his assiduity over and above his actual studies, may be graciously accepted by Your Electoral Grace. Connoisseurs and non-connoisseurs must candidly admit, from these present pieces, that Beethoven will in time fill the position of one of Europe's greatest composers, and I shall be proud to be able to speak of myself as his teacher; I only wish that he may remain with me a little while longer.

"While we are on the subject of Beethoven, Your Electoral Grace will perhaps permit me to say a few words concerning his financial status. For the past year he was allotted one hundred ducats. No doubt you yourself are convinced that this sum was insufficient, and not even enough to live on; undoubtedly Your Highness had his own reasons for sending him into the great world with such a paltry sum. In these circumstances, and to prevent him from falling into the hands of usurers, I have partly gone security for him and partly advanced cash, so that he owes me five hundred florins, of which not one penny has been spent without need. ... I think if Your Electoral Grace would send him a thousand florins for the coming year Your Highness would carry out your favor to him to the fullest extent and at the same time relieve all him of his distress. The teachers who are absolutely essential for him, and the display which is necessary if he is to gain admission into numerous salons, take so much of a thousand florins as to leave him only enough for the barest necessities.

"As for the extravagance which one fears will tempt any young man who goes into the great world, I think I can answer for that, for a hundred circumstances have confirmed me in my opinion that he is capable of sacrificing everything quite unconstrainedly for his art. . . . In the hope that Your Electoral Grace will continue his patronage of my dear pupil by graciously acceding to this my request, I am with profound respect,

Your Electoral Grace's most humble and obedient

Joseph Haydn,

Conductor to Prince Esterházy"

The ungracious Elector answered as follows:

"To Prince Esterházy's Conductor in Vienna, from Bonn, 23rd of December, 1793 —

"I received the music of the young Beethoven which you sent me together with your letter. Since, however, with the exception of the fugue, he composed and performed this music here in Bonn long before he undertook his second journey to Vienna, I cannot see that it indicates any evidence of his progress. . . . I do not see at all why his financial circumstances should be as reduced as you have indicated to me.

"I am wondering if he would not do better to begin his return journey, in order that he may once again to take up his post in my service; for I very much doubt whether he will have made any important progress in composition and taste during his present sojourn, and I fear he will only bring back debts from his journey, just as he did from his first trip to Vienna."

Beethoven stayed in Vienna, however, and the next year the Elector was turned out by the French Revolutionary army and his orchestra came to an end.

In the meanwhile Haydn was making plans for a second trip to England. Salomon wrote that he regretted that he could not come to meet him and accompany him to England as he had before, whereupon Haydn asked Beethoven, "How would the Grand Mogul like to go with me to London?"

Full of fierce pride, Beethoven refused the invitation, fearing he might be asked to act as valet for Haydn on the trip; he made some excuse for not accepting. Haydn decided to take with him his devoted servant, Johann Elssler, who also acted as his secretary and copyist. They set forth on January 19, 1794.

Now that Marianne Genzinger was gone, there was no longer anyone Haydn cared to write to about his daily activities in London. Instead he very carefully jotted down events in his diary, describing the warm welcome he received, how enthusiastically he was greeted by old friends, and how eagerly everyone waited to hear his new compositions. London was full of French aristocrats, refugees from the Revolution, and many of them attended Haydn's concerts and expressed their admiration so enthusiastically that a reporter for a German newspaper who was present at one concert complained that they spoiled the effect of the music, breaking in on it with their applause instead of waiting till the end. He wrote, "It is truly wonderful what sublime and august thoughts this master weaves into his works. Passages often occur that make it impossible to listen to them without becoming excited. We are altogether carried away by admiration and forced to applaud with hand and mouth. . . . In every symphony of Haydn the adagio or andante is sure to be repeated each time because of the enthusiastic desire for encores. The worthy Haydn, whose personal acquaintance I highly value, conducts himself on these occasions in the most modest manner. He is indeed a goodhearted, candid, honest man, esteemed and beloved by all."

Salomon was able to get outstanding soloists to play

under Haydn. Several helped with his benefit concert, and afterwards he played at theirs in return. He was also in great demand as a music teacher and was paid a guinea a lesson (about five dollars), which was a very respectable fee at that time.

As soon as the concert season was over, Haydn took the opportunity of making little trips around southern England. He went to Cowes, Newport, Winchester, Southampton, the Isle of Wight, Bath, and Bristol. He especially liked the beautiful cathedral at Winchester.

He returned to London in time for another season of concerts at which he would conduct his three new London Symphonies, Symphonies No. 102, 103, and 104, which were the tenth, eleventh, and twelfth of the symphonies he had undertaken to compose for Salomon's concerts. In these London Symphonies Haydn reached the summit of his art as a symphonic composer. They were like his character, clear, straightforward, fresh and winning, with a childlike cheerfulness that made the hearer feel that the composer wanted to make everyone happy with his music. They had amazing freedom and variety of form.

Many of Haydn's symphonies had special names attached to them for one reason or another. The "Miracle" Symphony, No. 96, was so called because of an incident at the first performance. The enthusiastic London audience left their seats to come forward and applaud Haydn. Just as they had left their seats, a huge chandelier from the ceiling crashed on the empty seats, and because the audience believed the symphony had saved the lives of the people who would have been in those seats if it had been just an ordinary symphony, they cried, "Miracle! Miracle!"

The "Military" Symphony, No. 100, was so called because in the second and fourth movements there is a battery consisting of big drum, cymbal, and triangle with kettledrums. The "Clock" Symphony, No. 101, was called this because of the tick-tocking Andante. The "Drumroll" Symphony, No. 103, because it opens with a long roll from the solo kettledrum. The "Surprise" Symphony, No. 94, was so named because of a tremendously loud chord crashing into a soft repetition of a staccato theme. It was said that Haydn put in this sudden bang so it would wake up the ladies in the audience.

In February, 1795, Haydn was introduced to the King of England. This was the same George III who was king at the time of the American Revolution. He had more or less given up trying to rule personally since the loss of the colonies, and in his old age he was popular. A musician who was present when Haydn was introduced to him solemnly recorded the occasion.

"The Duke of York gave a grand concert of instrumental music at York House, at which their Majesties and the Princesses were present. Salomon led the band and Haydn presided at the pianoforte. At the end of the first part of the concert Haydn had the distinguished honor of being formally introduced to his Majesty, George III, by the Prince of Wales. My station at the time was so near to the king that I could not avoid hearing the whole of their conversation. Among other observations, his Majesty said: 'Dr. Haydn, you have written a good deal.' Haydn modestly replied: 'Yes, Sire, a great deal more than is good.' His Majesty neatly rejoined: 'Oh, no, the world contradicts that.' After his introduction, at the Queen's desire, Haydn sat down to the pianoforte and, surrounded by her Majesty and her daughters, sang and accompanied himself admirably in several of his canzonets."

When the Prince of Wales entertained his father at Carlton House, he had Haydn conduct a concert, mostly of his own music; and the Queen invited him to a number of musical evenings at Buckingham House. She was one of the many people who would have liked to persuade him to stay in England and make his home there as Handel had done; but Haydn wanted to go back to Vienna.

Before Haydn left London a benefit concert was given in his honor, after which he received many parting gifts. Among them was a beautiful silver goblet, its cup made from a coconut, which was a present from Clementi, the musician and composer. A red and green parrot which was taught to say, "Come, Papa Haydn!" was presented to him by an ardent admirer.

Haydn had been a great social success as well as a musical success. He knew how to pay homage to ladies; the men liked him because of his sharp wit, his interest in horseracing, fishing, shooting, and good wine. The musicians who played with him respected him as a great composer but also loved him because of his gentleness and good nature; they liked it when he called them his "dear children," coaxing them to play their very best by his kindness, rather than bullying them with severe commands. Haydn left many good friends behind him in England.

He carried home, besides many gifts, a large sum of money and a great number of new compositions. His self-confidence had grown so much in London that he realized that from now on he would be less sensitive to what the Viennese critics, who still thought of him chiefly as the conductor of a rich Hungarian nobleman, might say or not say about him.

He no longer cared what they said. He knew his own worth; his inspiration had been fired into a great blaze by his dazzling success in England. His vitality was nourished by the admiration and esteem he found there, and his gratitude was shown in the creation of the twelve great London Symphonies.

*Chapter Fifteen*

IN VIENNA, Haydn found that his London symphonies were becoming well known. He appeared at several concerts and gave one in which he directed his three latest London symphonies. He had received a more remarkable recognition of his greatness from Count Harrach, the son of his father's landlord, who was so proud of the famous musician who had been born in his territory that he put up a monument to him. In the autumn after Haydn's return from England, Count Harrach invited him to Rohrau to see the monument and revisit his old home. Count Harrach and a party of noble admirers drove from Vienna with him. Haydn was much gratified with the monument — a square pillar surmounting three stone steps with a handsome

inscription to him as well as his portrait bust in marble —
and very much moved to see again the dear old cottage.

Prince Anton had died soon after Haydn left for
England, and the new prince, another Nicholas, was eager to
be a magnificent patron of the arts like his grandfather.
"You'll have to hurry to get a good orchestra and put it in
shape for a first performance in my town palace in January,"
he told Haydn. "Perhaps you are not aware that I am not
as fond of Esterháza as my grandfather was. I plan to use
Eisenstadt in the summer and to spend the winters in
Vienna."

"I will do my best to have the orchestra ready in time,
Your Highness," said Haydn. He was glad to hear that there
would be no question of going back into his wilderness at
Esterháza. He had a nice little house at Eisenstadt, and he
had bought the house in the suburb of Vienna that Maria
Anna had found and was having all sorts of things done to
it and delightedly looking forward to spending winters in
the city. He would hate to be buried in the country again,
far away from all the interesting things going on in Vienna.

It did not take long for Haydn to discover that the
new Prince was the least pleasant of the four he had worked
for, not only because he was not much interested in instrumental works, preferring church music to any other form
of composition, but because of his lack of musical understanding and his rude and haughty manner.

One day at a rehearsal of the orchestra, Prince Nicholas made what Haydn considered an unjustified criticism and suggestion. "Your Highness," said Haydn firmly, "this is something for *me* to decide."

The indignant Prince left the room abruptly; the musicians were horrified at their conductor's audacity and wondered what would happen to them now. The Prince's wife, however, who admired Haydn and was fond of him, told him after this incident, "I do hope you have not been too much offended by my husband."

Haydn could not hold back a flow of grievances. Among other things, he told the Princess that his salary was too small and that he was not treated respectfully by the Prince. She said, "I will see to it that your wage is increased and that in the future you are addressed as 'Dr. Haydn' instead of just as 'Haydn.' "

"Thank you, Your Highness. It is a great privilege to have you as my friend."

It was now Haydn's chief duty to compose church music for the Prince, and six of his loveliest masses were composed for Prince Nicholas's name-day in the Septembers from 1796 to 1802.

While he worked on the "Kettledrum" mass, in the summer of 1796, the Imperial armies in Italy were collapsing under the skillful attacks of a young French general, Napoleon. The music laments the dead, and we hear the sound of drums and trumpets, giving the feeling of exaltation and confidence despite death and disaster. The "Nelson" mass was composed two years later, when Admiral Nelson had destroyed Napoleon's fleet at the Battle of the Nile. In 1800 it was played for Nelson himself when he visited Eisenstadt.

On festive occasions the Prince liked to show off his famous conductor, who added greatly to the reputation of the noble household; but one day Haydn asked him to have a member of the orchestra conduct the ordinary concerts at the palace, explaining, "I should like to have time to write a work which may give permanent fame to my name in the world." Ever since hearing Handel's oratorios in London, particularly *The Messiah,* Haydn had felt inspired to try his hand at an oratorio. He had chosen for a subject the Bible story of the Creation and had been given an English oratorio text based on the Bible and on the description of the Creation in Milton's *Paradise Lost.*

Such a large work would take a long time to complete, and there was no telling how the expenses of performing it properly would be met. But the worry about expense was soon dispelled. The curator of the Vienna Court Library, Baron van Swieten, persuaded twelve music-loving aristocrats to promise to contribute fifty ducats each in order to guarantee the expenses of a performance when the time came, and to provide a small payment for the composer. Van Swieten had done a great deal to introduce Handel's work to the

Viennese music lovers. He had been Haydn's friend and admirer — and Mozart's, when Mozart was alive — for a long time. Now he wrote the German oratorio text of *The Creation* for Haydn, translating and adapting the English one and using the words of the German Bible whenever he could.

How happily Haydn worked on the oratorio, finding descriptive tones and melody for the sounds and the beauty of nature! "Never was I so devout as when composing *The Creation,*" Haydn said later. "I knelt down every day and prayed to God to strengthen me for my work." He also prayed when he found his inspiration flagging, rising from the pianoforte to say a rosary. He never found this method to fail.

It took Haydn more than a year and a half to finish *The Creation.* Its first performance was arranged for April, 1798, in Prince Schwarzenberg's palace. The aristocrats and the most important musical and literary people of Vienna were invited to hear the oratorio in sumptuous surroundings. Haydn conducted *The Creation* with a baton. Salieri, the court composer, played the piano; and the singers and members of the orchestra were the best to be had.

The dramatic music made one feel and see as well as hear the beauty of Nature, the sweetness of the south wind, the happiness of sunlight; it made one believe in God and man. In the first part there is lightning, rolling thunder, and mist that becomes rain. "The dreary, wasteful hail" beats down, after which the snow falls, quiet and mysterious. There are grand choruses to confirm the individual works of the Creation, and when the final chorus in the first part proclaims, "The Heavens are telling the Glory of God," one feels the radiant sun and sees the color of the world in resplendent hues, the angels of heaven looking down on the mountains, meadows, brooks, rivers, and seas.

In the second part comes the creation of the beasts. There are songs such as "Cheerful roaring stands the tawny lion" and "The nimble stag bears up his branching head," "Upheaved from the deep th'immense Leviathan," and "The eagle soaring higher and higher into the sky, writing with mighty plumes." Haydn described the shimmering, swarming, humming hordes of insects and creeping worms. So fresh is the music that it is as if we were seeing these creatures for the first time. In the third part, Adam and Eve sing the praises of the newly created world. (The singers in the first two parts are angels.)

The success of the oratorio was stupendous, far above anything Haydn had ever dreamed of. The audience was thunderous in its applause. Haydn felt humble as well as exalted at the triumph of his new large work. He had taken the greatest pains to make this composition something people would enjoy, something he could be proud of. And he had succeeded beyond belief.

All the newspapers notices were rapturous. It was not only the musically educated who were enthusiastic about *The Creation,* but the common people as well. A widely read popular magazine, *Eipeldauer's Letters,* written in Viennese dialect, said of one performance, "When the music began there was instantly such a silence that you could have heard a little mouse run; and had people not clapped their hands you would have thought that no one at all was in the theater. But, my dear, I shall never hear such beautiful music again in my life. I should not have been sorry if I had been forced to sit three hours more . . . I should never have believed that the human bellows, the gut of sheep, and the skin of calves could produce such miracles. The music alone expressed thunder and lightning, and you could hear the shower of rain and the new water, and the birds really sang and the lion roared, and you could really hear how the worms creep in the earth. In short, I never left a theater so delighted and I dreamed the whole night of the creation of the world."

The Church, however, was definitely offended by certain parts of the great work. It had too much gaiety and jollity in it, too many comic effects for a religious work. Among the poets and writers there was disagreement. Schiller denounced the oratorio, Goethe championed it. Haydn's own answer to the criticism that his church compositions were too gay was, "Well, I cannot help it. I give forth what is in me. When I think of the Divine Being my heart is so full of joy that the notes fly off as from a spindle, and as I have a cheerful heart, He will pardon me if I serve Him cheerfully."

Besides working on *The Creation,* Haydn had been composing masses, a trumpet concerto, a number of string quartets, and trios for the piano. He also composed a national anthem for his country. He had often heard "God Save the King" while he was in England, and he felt that Austria needed a good national anthem too. On the Emperor's birthday in February, 1797, the new anthem was sung in his honor in all the theaters of Vienna, and it was a resounding success. The Emperor sent a gold box with his picture on it to Haydn as a token of gratitude, and the new hymn was played and sung all over Vienna. The tune is the "Austria" of the hymn books; it is often used for English hymns.

In the beginning of 1797 Haydn finally moved into his own house in a quiet suburb of Vienna. It was the house Maria Anna had found, but Maria Anna had been in bad health for a long time, and now she lived mainly in Baden, a health resort where there were baths for her rheumatism. Baden was a pleasant place: Haydn had sent his brother Hansl there summer after summer, and Mozart had sent his wife there when she was not well.

Honors began pouring in to Haydn even before the great success of *The Creation.* Sweden notified him that he had been made a member of the Royal Music Academy. Even the Society of Musicians in Vienna, which had refused his application for membership in 1778, now offered him membership without fee. Haydn was delighted to be recognized at last, and in gratitude offered to conduct a program of his church music and other compositions for the benefit of the poor families of musicians.

From Paris came a medal with his portrait and a letter sent by one hundred and forty-two French musicians who had performed *The Creation*.

The letter said, "The French artists, gathered together in the Théatre des Arts to perform that immortal work, the 'Creation of the World,' composed by the celebrated Haydn, are filled with a just admiration for his genius and beg him to accept the homage of their respect, of the enthusiasm which inspired them, and of the medal which they have had struck in his honor.

"No year goes by in which a new product of this composer does not enchant the artists, enlighten their minds, contribute to the progress of the art, widen the immense spaces of harmony, and prove that its expanses are boundless if one follows the luminous torch with which Haydn has brilliantly illuminated the present which points the way to the future. But the imposing conception of the ORATORIO even surpasses, if such a thing be possible, everything which this wise composer has hitherto offered to an astonished Europe.

"When in this work Haydn imitates the FIRE OF HEAVEN, he seems to have portrayed himself, and thus persuades us all that his name will shine as long as the stars whose rays he seems to have absorbed.

"P.S.: If we here admire the skill and talent by means of which Citizen GATTEAUX [the sculptor] has so well reflected our intentions in the engraving of the medal we offer to Haydn, we must also pay tribute to the loftiness of the sculptor's sentiments, for he has been content to receive for his efforts merely the glory which is his today."

Napoleon had been present to hear *The Creation*, and it was said that his life had been saved because he had gone to hear Haydn's oratorio instead of carrying out his original plan to go to a service at Notre Dame. A cart filled with explosives had been placed on his route to the cathedral to be blown up when he passed. But Napoleon had decided at the last moment to go to hear *The Creation* instead.

Haydn's devoted servant, Johann Elssler, wrote an account of his master's daily activities during these years. "In the summertime he rose at 6:30 a.m. First he shaved, which he did for himself up to his seventy-third year, and then he finished dressing. If a pupil was present, he had to play his lesson on the piano while the master dressed. All mistakes were promptly corrected and a new task was set. This took an hour and a half. At eight o'clock sharp, breakfast had to be on the table, and immediately after breakfast Haydn sat down at the piano, improvising and drafting the sketches of some composition.

"From 8 to 11:30 his time was taken up in this way. At 11:30 calls were received or made, or he went for a walk until 1:30. The hour from 2 to 3 was reserved for dinner, after which Haydn immediately did some little work in the house or resumed his musical occupations. He scored the morning's sketches, devoting three to four hours to this. At 8 p.m. Haydn usually went out, and at 9 he came home and sat down to write a score or he took a book and read until 10 p.m.

"At that time he had supper, which consisted of bread and wine. Haydn made a rule of eating nothing but bread and wine at night and infringed it only on sundry occasions when he was invited to supper. He liked gay conversation and some merry entertainment at the table. At 11:30 he went to bed, in his old age even later. Wintertime made no difference to the schedule, except that Haydn got up a half hour later."

His brother Michael came to Vienna to visit him, and this was a happy time for Haydn. Michael asked if he were planning to compose another oratorio.

"I'm not sure, Michael. Baron van Swieten urges me to compose an oratorio based on *The Seasons* by the English poet, Thomson. He says it is a perfect subject for an oratorio and that he will make a libretto for me from the poem. He gives me absolutely no peace about it and insists that I begin composing right away. He enjoys telling me how to go about it, what instruments to use to describe the way frogs hop about and all that kind of thing. After the disparaging remarks about the way I used the sounds of nature in *The Creation,* I am not very keen on exposing myself to ridicule again."

"I shouldn't pay the slightest attention to what those idiots say. Go ahead with *The Seasons.* You'll make it as wonderful a masterpiece as *The Creation,* I'm sure."

"Perhaps I'll do it some day, but my heart is not really in it now."

Haydn had felt the strain of composing *The Creation.* He was ill after it was finished, and in the spring of 1800 he was quite seriously ill. He recovered, however, and was able to go to Buda, the capital of Hungary, to conduct *The Creation.* He did not feel up to going to Paris to conduct the first performance there, and so the French musicians had to be content with honoring him from a distance.

When he came back from Buda, Haydn received word that Maria Anna had died at Baden. She had been there so long that her death did not make a difference in his daily life. He had a pleasant household with servants who admired and loved him and played cards with him in the evening and who took very good care of him. Poor Maria Anna with her bad health and her bad temper had had a very unhappy life, and her death probably did not make anyone very sad.

Haydn was working on the new oratorio, but somehow it went far less easily than *The Creation*. His heart wasn't in it, and he forced himself to compose. Never had he labored over a composition as he did on this one, never were there so many difficulties to overcome. He felt his health giving way under the strain of it all and complained to Elssler, "I think *The Seasons* will finish *me* off before I finish *it*."

"Please don't say that, Master. It will be as great a work as your *Creation*. You are doing in the oratorios what Mozart did in his great operas."

When, at long last, the new oratorio was completed, Prince Schwarzenberg again lent his palace for its first performance. The audience, as distinguished as the first audience of *The Creation,* was overcome by the freshness and idyllic quality of the music, the beautiful tonal descriptions of Spring, Summer, Autumn, and Winter. In *The Creation,* God was the chief personage; but in *The Seasons,* the four seasons govern all the actions and thoughts of men and beasts. In "Spring," the earth seems to free itself from Winter; then the weather changes suddenly to wintry violence; following this, Spring slips in with the song, "Come, gentle Spring."

The plowman goes forth into the fields, noises of the countryside are heard, the bleat of lambs and other small animals. In "Summer," Haydn celebrates the heat of the sun and its power on all living things with the song, "Hail, thou glorious sun, thou source of light and life!"

There are thunderstorms as in *The Creation,* and this time such howling storms that it is as if Haydn had summoned up his last and greatest powers.

The critics wrote in the newspapers, "With what reverence and boundless enthusiasm the audience listened to the powerful visions of *The Seasons!* The abundance of splendid ideas surprised and overwhelmed the boldest expectations."

The new oratorio was such a huge success that the Empress, who had studied singing with some of the best teachers, asked for a performance of *The Seasons* at court, to be followed the next day by *The Creation.* Afterwards Haydn wrote to Michael, "The Empress sang the soprano solos in both oratorios with much taste and expression, though in a small voice."

A few days later the public was permitted to hear *The Seasons* in a public hall, and it was as great a triumph as *The Creation,* bringing Haydn high acclaim and a good sum of money. An admirer came to congratulate him, saying "This is even greater than *The Creation";* but to this Haydn answered, "Don't you realize that in the one, angels are singing, in the other, merely rustics?" There is magnificent music in every part of *The Seasons,* but Haydn never believed in it as strongly as he did in *The Creation.*

*Chapter Sixteen*

HAYDN FELT very weak after finishing *The Seasons,* and that summer he worked on his will. He had a great many people to leave money to, for though he had left his father's house in Rohrau when he was only five years old and hardly knew what it was like to grow up in a family, among sisters and brothers, he felt very close to all his relatives, near and distant, and had a deep affection for them. He made a number of charitable bequests, and he left his large gold medal from Paris to Prince Nicholas Esterházy and a smaller one to the Count von Harrach; but the bulk of his will was taken up with a large number of bequests to individual relatives and friends and servants. Haydn was the only member of his family who had risen to wealth, and he had no children of his own; it gave him great pleasure to be a generous uncle to his sisters' children and grandchildren and to stand godfather to the children of his relatives and of the Esterházy musicians. Now he carefully divided up his property among the numerous humble smiths and cooks and seamstresses who were his cherished relatives — not forgetting, of course, his musician brothers Hansl and Michael.

The three brothers were together in the autumn of 1801. Michael had lost his property and his job when the French invaded Salzburg, but his brother helped him and the musical world of Vienna made much of him. He was quite a distinguished church composer, and both the Empress and Prince Nicholas Esterházy gave him large commissions.

Prince Nicholas had noticed that Haydn was not in his usual good health, and he suggested, "Perhaps it would lighten your duties if we could persuade your brother Michael to assist you. As you know, I am chiefly interested in church music."

"It would be a great help to me, Your Highness, and a great personal pleasure," said Haydn. Michael, too, was pleased; but by now Salzburg was home to him, and what he really hoped for was that the Salzburg orchestra should be revived. He enjoyed his visit to Vienna and Eisenstadt, but afterwards he went back home.

The Prince had been certain that he would accept

without hesitation. He sent Michael a letter in January, saying, "Since I do not doubt that you have already made most of the preparations incident to your coming and settling here without further delay, I shall await your arrival with pleasure; and as a sign of your attention, I expect to receive from you by August, at the latest, a *missa solemnis* and a *vesper de beata*."

Although Michael wrote in February that he would ask permission to leave Salzburg in June or July to enter the Prince's service in August, he saw in the end that he was too attached to Salzburg to leave it. He was sorry when the Prince withdrew his offer, but his brother Joseph thought that he was too straightforward for a courtier and that he probably would not have been happy working for Prince Nicholas.

Nicholas Esterházy was not accustomed to being disappointed in his wishes, and he was surprised as well as ruffled by Michael's reluctance to leave Salzburg. Haydn tried to appease him, and a few years later recommended another Assistant Conductor, Hummel, who had been a pupil of Mozart's.

Hummel was delighted at the offer and lost no time in accepting it and coming to Eisenstadt. But soon Haydn saw trouble brewing between the musicians of the orchestra and the new conductor. Hummel was so tactless and brusque in handling the men, so lacking in kindliness, that the musicians begged Haydn, "Please do not leave your children, Papa Haydn. We need you."

"Be patient, dear ones. Do not make it hard for Hummel by being disgruntled and not cooperating. If it were not for my failing health, I would not leave you to other conductors, I assure you."

The faithful Elssler was distressed by Haydn's growing weakness. He could no longer leave the house for a stroll, and he began to have difficulty in walking alone to the piano to work on his compositions. When Elssler mentioned the concert that was to be given in celebration of Haydn's seventy-third birthday, Haydn said, "I am afraid I will not have the strength to go to it. Come, help me take a short walk in the garden; there are signs of spring everywhere. I'll have to lean on you a bit, my legs are so badly swollen. Ah, my friend, there is not much strength left in me."

"No, no, sir. Why I just saw you working on another quartet."

"Yes, I have finished two movements of it, but I doubt if I shall ever get the other two completed. There is one thing I must do before I leave this world."

"What is that, sir?" asked Elssler anxiously.

"I want to draw up a list of all the compositions which I can remember having completed from my eighteenth until my seventy-third year; it will represent fifty-five years of work. Otherwise I may forget my own compositions.

I'll dictate what I remember to you, and you write it down. Perhaps we'll begin tomorrow."

"Gladly, sir, whenever you desire."

And so they began spending a few hours on the list every day. Elssler saw that Haydn was beginning to forget what he had composed. Sometimes by mistake he included a composition which was not his, or omitted one of his own until reminded. At last, when they considered the list complete, Haydn looked it over and was surprised himself to see the enormous amount he had done:

One hundred and four symphonies, twenty-four operas and overtures, five marches, eighty dances, five piano concertos, four violin concertos, eighty-four string quartets, two cello concertos, two horn concertos, one for trumpet, dozens of baryton concertos, two duo sonatas for violin and viola, one hundred and twenty-six trios for baryton, viola, and cello, nine trios for two flutes and cello, six quartets for flute, viola, and cello, twenty-five divertimenti, fifty-two piano sonatas, thirty-two pieces for musical clocks, twenty-one trios for two violins and cello with piano, thirty-one piano trios, twelve masses, thirty-three smaller church compositions, two oratorios, choral cantatas, and over two hundred and fifty arrangements of Scotch and Welsh songs.

"I am sure there are other compositions, sir, which we have not yet remembered," said Elssler.

"Well, we'll put them down when we think of them,"

said Haydn wearily. *"Sunt mala mixta bonis;* some of my children are well-bred, some ill-bred, and here and there is a changeling among them."

Everywhere the interest in Haydn's compositions continued to such a degree that when it became known that he was in declining health, rumors began spreading through Europe about it; in some places it was actually thought that he had died. There was great consternation about this; letters and obituary notices appeared in papers, and a memorial concert was arranged in Paris at which Mozart's *Requiem* would be performed. The Viennese papers quickly quelled the rumors, and at the good news that Haydn was not dead after all, the concert was called off.

Haydn's Scotch publisher, George Thomson, was much distressed at the rumor of his death and wrote from Edinburgh to commiserate with Elssler. Weak though he was, Haydn could not resist answering the letter himself, saying, "I am very much alive still. No doubt you heard about the proposed memorial concert in Paris. The good gentlemen! I am greatly indebted to them for the unusual honor. Had I only known of it in time, I would have traveled to Paris to conduct the requiem myself!"

Yes, he was alive and thankful to be alive, ailing though he was. He wished he did not feel so weak, that he had the strength to go to the piano and work on his compositions. There were still so many tunes running around in his

*152*

head. He said, "Musical ideas pursue me to the point of torture. I cannot get rid of them; they stand before me like a wall. If it is an allegro that pursues me, my pulse beats faster, I cannot sleep; if it is an adagio, I find my pulse beating slowly. My imagination plays upon me as if I were a keyboard."

To Griesinger, a friend, he had said, "I have by no means exhausted my talent; ideas are often floating in my mind and I could have carried my art far beyond anything it has yet attained, if my physical powers were equal to my task."

His creative talent gave him no rest. "If only I could put down on paper the tunes that plague me and free myself of them," he said to Elssler. "I have only just learned in my old age how to use the wind instruments, and now that I do understand them, I must leave the world."

"Dear Master, I wish I could write down your compositions for you. But all I am fit for is to copy them."

"And a good and accurate copyist you have been. Your copies even look like mine. By the way, is anyone coming to see me today?"

"Yes, sir, the Czech musician, Herr Tomaschek."

"Well, then, you had better help me get dressed neatly. My dear mother trained me so well that it has become second nature for me to be tidy, even though I am an invalid."

When the visitor arrived he found Haydn sitting in

an arm chair very much dressed up. Afterwards he wrote down an account of his call on the great man, including a careful account of his costume: "He wore a powdered wig with sidelocks, a white neckband with a gold buckle, a white richly embroidered waistcoat of heavy silk in the midst of which shone a splendid jabot; his dress coat was of fine coffee-colored cloth with embroidered cuffs, black silk breeches, white silk hose, shoes with large silver buckles curved over the instep; on the little table next to him lay a pair of white kid gloves as if he were ready to go out." Powdered wigs were old-fashioned now, but many older men refused to give up a fashion that had lasted longer than they could remember.

Haydn greeted his caller warmly, chatted with him awhile, and opened the special box beside him which contained the medals sent him as honors from various countries. These were the visible signs of his success at home and abroad. He took great pleasure in them and in the memory of his English visits.

When Mozart's name was mentioned, Haydn burst into tears and said, "How I loved and admired that young genius! I never heard one of his compositions without learning something from it."

Almost every day devoted friends came to see Haydn. The Princess Esterházy often came, and she offered him the use of a carriage whenever he wished to take an outing.

In March, 1808, as Haydn's seventy-sixth birthday drew near, there was to be a performance of *The Creation* in the great hall of the university. Before his friends told him about it, they had to consult his doctor to make sure he was well enough to honor the concert with his presence.

Since the weather was mild, the doctor gave Haydn permission to leave the house for the occasion. He was taken to the concert in Prince Esterházy's carriage. At the university he found such a crowd waiting outside to enter the concert hall, or just standing to stare at the celebrities, that a military guard had to be called out.

The highest nobility, the most distinguished musicians, greeted Haydn as he was carried in an armchair, because of his swollen legs, into the beautiful hall. On his silk coat hung the treasured gold medal from Paris.

As Haydn entered there was a flourish of drums and trumpets and shouts of "Long live Haydn!" His chair was placed next to that of the Princess Esterházy; she watched over him anxiously, and when she noticed that he was shivering with excitement and emotion, she quickly wrapped her shawl over his frail shoulders. Other noble ladies, seeing this, also offered their costly shawls, proud to have them touching the great man.

Before the music began, poems praising Haydn and his music were given to him. Then Salieri, the court composer, rose to conduct the oratorio. There was a hush among the audience as the singers and the orchestra began: "In the beginning God created the heaven and the earth; and the earth was without form, and void; and darkness was upon the face of the deep. And the Spirit of God moved upon the face of the waters. And God said, Let there be light; and there was light."

At this point the audience broke into applause. With trembling hands uplifted, Haydn said, "Not from me — it all comes from above."

"And God saw the light, that it was good: and God divided the light from darkness," continued the oratorio.

At the intermission, people rushed to congratulate and embrace Haydn. They shook his hand, praised his magnificent music. Beethoven knelt humbly before him and kissed the hands and forehead of his old teacher. Haydn was particularly affected by Beethoven's affection and tribute and said, "So, Grand Mogul, I see that at last you are willing to bend the knee."

"Yes, my dear Master, for your great music I am not too proud to do so."

Haydn was taken home before he grew over-tired from the press of admirers and friends; it was feared the strain and excitement would be too much for him.

At home he said to Elssler, "What a great day in my life this has been! And to think that even that stubborn genius, Beethoven, did me the honor of kneeling before me

and kissing me. I shall never forget it, never."

In 1809 the French were at war with Austria again. Soon Napoleon's army had taken the western suburbs of Vienna. They were making their headquarters in the castle at Schönbrunn, and Napoleon ordered a tremendous bombardment of Vienna on May 12th. A cannon ball fell so near Haydn's house that it shook as if there were an earthquake. The servants and one of Haydn's grand-nieces, who had come to look after him, were terrified. Haydn, however, remained calm and said, "Don't be frightened, dear children. Where Haydn is, nothing can happen to you."

Nevertheless, as the bombardment continued, the effect on Haydn's nervous system and ebbing strength was great. Then Vienna was occupied by French troops. One day a French officer, Sulemy, appeared at the door and asked to see Doctor Haydn. Afraid to refuse, Elssler let him in. The Frenchman greeted Haydn with great respect and said, "I have come to pay tribute to the great composer of *The Creation*. I know it so thoroughly that I can sing many of the songs in it."

Haydn said, "It would be a pleasure to hear you," and Sulemy sang "In Native Worth" so well that the old composer was greatly moved.

After the visitor had left, Haydn suddenly told Elssler that he felt like playing the piano again, and asked to be carried to it. Three times he played the Austrian National

Anthem which he had composed twelve years ago; into his playing he put everything he felt for his unhappy country, so near collapse now. When he finished, he turned to Elssler and his grand-niece. "I played that very expressively, didn't I? I even surprised myself."

The next day and the next he stayed in bed, dozing off from time to time, the kindly expression on his face no different from usual. Shortly after midnight on May 29 he fell asleep and never woke again. It was just two months after his seventy-seventh birthday. He was born in the same year as George Washington, in 1732, and died the year Lincoln was born, in 1809.

Because of the war with France and the upheaval and disorganization in Vienna, the news of Haydn's death was hardly noticed and the funeral took place without any special ceremonies.

But two weeks later there was an official funeral service. Members of the French army alternated with the Austrian city grenadiers to form a line around the catafalque, the black-draped platform where Haydn's body had rested before it was buried. His medals were placed there, and a little ivory tablet engraved with his name which had been given to him in London as a free pass to all London concerts. Mozart's *Requiem* was played.

Seeing high-ranking French officials and army officers joining with the cultured world of Vienna and with crowds of humble Viennese citizens to give homage to a great composer, the Viennese whispered to each other, "Even our enemies have united with us in honoring our Joseph Haydn."

Salomon mourned Haydn as if he had been his cherished brother. The tablet over his grave in Westminster Abbey says simply, "Johann Peter Salomon, born 1745, died 1815. He brought Haydn to England in 1791 and 1794."

What Salomon had done for music in bringing Haydn to London was worthy of celebration. The two visits to England aroused Haydn's enthusiasm to such a pitch, stimulated and inspired him so much, that he composed some of his greatest music, the exquisite result of his happiness among the English people.

On Haydn's tombstone is incised in Latin a line from the Psalms: "Die I shall not, but live and proclaim the works of the Lord."

And so it is, for his music has spread over the world like a marvelous blessing to make us happy and glad we are alive.

jB
Haydn

c.1

Mirsky
Haydn

Date Due

|  |  |  |  |
|--|--|--|--|
|  |  |  |  |
|  |  |  |  |
|  |  |  |  |
|  |  |  |  |
|  |  |  |  |
|  |  |  |  |
|  |  |  |  |
|  |  |  |  |
|  |  |  |  |
|  |  |  |  |
|  |  |  |  |

NEW YORK MILLS PUBLIC LIBRARY
NEW YORK MILLS, NEW YORK